MY LIFE AS I REMEMBER IT

By Pete Shubin

Ignite Press
Fresno, CA

Copyright © 2020, Peter M. Shubin

All rights reserved. No part of this book may be used or reproduced by any means, graphic, electronic, or mechanical (including any information storage retrieval system) without the express written permission from the author, except in the case of brief quotations for use in articles and reviews wherein appropriate attribution of the source is made.

Published in the United States by Ignite Press.
ignitepress.us

ISBN: 978-1-953655-08-0 (Amazon Print)
ISBN: 978-1-953655-09-7 (IngramSpark) Paperback
ISBN: 978-1-953655-10-3 (Ebook)

Because of the dynamic nature of the Internet, web addresses or links contained in this book may have been changed since publication and may no longer be valid. The content of this book and all expressed opinions are those of the author and do not reflect the publisher or the publishing team. The author is solely responsible for all content included herein.

Cover design by Salman Sarwar

This book is dedicated to my Mom and Dad. You gave me the best education I could have gotten, one that money cannot buy. You sent me through the University of Hard Knocks, the same school that you went through.

Pete's parents

ACKNOWLEDGMENTS

First and foremost, I want to acknowledge my beautiful wife, Charlesia, who has been so lovingly patient with me throughout twenty-five years of marriage.

I also want to acknowledge Goodyear Tire and Rubber Company. Although I have experienced a lot of conflict with that company, it is through them that I had my pathway to success.

I also want to thank some of my oldest and most loyal employees, who have helped with the success of Goodguys Tire and Auto Repair. *Thanks* to Joey Ingalls, whom I consider a genius in the field of technicians. *Thanks* to George Navarro, whom I hired on a collect phone call in 1977, and who is still with me and will take an assignment wherever he is sent. (I will never forget that phone call, when you called as a complete stranger and told me you wanted to come and interview for a job, but you needed to borrow from me the money for gas!) *Thanks* to Janice Park, my controller for more than twenty years, who was such a big help to me in setting up my administrative office in a responsible way. *Thanks* to Paul Seta, who came to work for me in 1991 and told me this would be the last job of his career. *Thanks* to John Cuevas, who stands out as the best technician in Fresno. *Thanks* to Tia Vang, my controller and office manager. *Thanks* to Pat Murray, who was hired to work in the warehouse but took over computer operations and has done a great job. *Thanks* to Ted Starkel for working with me through that antiquated accounting system which Goodyear had. *Thanks* to Harrison Mills, my payroll and human relations manager. *Thanks* to John Brownrigg, who has been running his business under my Management Program since 1992. *Thanks* to Armen Petrosyan, who also became a franchisee in my Program in 2010. *Thanks* to Kelly Kolb, who has never directly worked for me, but who on my recommendation works for Scott as a store supervisor. Last, but far from least, *thanks* to my son, Scott Shubin, who wanted to be a chiropractor but decided it would be easier to come and work for me. Scott is doing an excellent job running his own business now.

Without any one of these people, Goodguys would not have achieved the same success.

TABLE OF CONTENTS

Foreword ix
Preface xiii
Introduction xv

1. Welcome to America! 1
2. Los Angeles 7
3. Growing Up on A Farm 15
4. Drifting from My Roots 23
5. Out on My Own 29
6. Falling in Love 33
7. Career Momentum 39
8. Getting Started in Fresno 43
9. Mike and Roxie 51
10. The Madera Store 55
11. Expanding 59
12. Mother 67
13. An Independent Tire Dealer 73
14. Legal Mess 79
15. Goodguys 85
16. The Mid-Eighties 91
17. Sadness at Home 97

18. Losing Reneé. 107
19. Life After Reneé 113
20. Management Agreement Program 121
21. Charlesia. 125
22. A New Venture 133
23. Some Vacations with Charlesia 141
24. More Vacations with Charlesia 147
25. Selling Stores. 153
26. Problems with Goodyear 159
27. Mario Andretti Comes to Fresno 167
28. Back in Love with Goodyear 175
29. End of The Road with Goodyear 181
30. Moving On 185
31. Shubin Family Reunion 193
32. A Big Surprise for Charlesia 205
33. The Silver Anniversary 213
34. A Long Way from Rahmatabad! 219

FOREWORD

I was the president of Bridgestone/Firestone when I met Pete Shubin at a conference in Mexico. From the minute we met, I liked his straight-shooting and fun-loving style. The more I learned about him, the more I admired him as a person and a businessman. He had fought his way to the top without losing his warm hearted and down to earth character. In my kind of business, I meet a lot of people, including just about every Bridgestone/Firestone dealer in the country. But Pete is one of those guys who became a good and long-time friend, as well as a business associate. I would like to talk a little about why that is, and why I believe Pete's book is worth a busy reader's time.

In the business world, there are two roads. Pete and I both started from the bottom in Firestone stores, but we chose different avenues in our climb. I went up the corporate ladder, where I needed to work hard and be good at what I did, but as a worker in a corporation I always had a guaranteed paycheck. Times could be good, or times could be bad, but Bridgestone/Firestone would always have money for my salary. Pete, on the other hand, chose the road of entrepreneurship. Starting from scratch, he built his own businesses, meaning he had no corporate cushion to fall back on if things got rough. I can imagine the nights he went to bed unsure of how he was going to pay his bills and employees the next day. The road of entrepreneurship is loaded with risk, and I take off my hat to those few who succeed.

I also admire people who start at the bottom and work their way up by relying not only on hard work and good intelligence, but also on character and principle. When I came with Mario Andretti to Fresno to help promote Goodguys and Bridgestone/Firestone products, I was able to tour some of the stores Pete has built, and to talk with employees who have stayed with him for decades. My experience enables me to identify what makes some business leaders stand out from others, and one of those characteristics is the ability to retain quality workers for long-term employment. This kind of loyalty from employees requires more than just providing a fair paycheck. If you want to learn about what else is required, I urge you to read Pete's story.

If you make the choice to walk with Pete Shubin through his life as he remembers it, you will read more than a story about savvy business decisions in the competitive tire and auto-repair industry. You will also learn how the challenging experiences in his personal life helped to develop his sensitivity toward others, and how this enabled him to see his employees not just as workers who do a job for a paycheck, but as complete people who should be treated with honesty and fairness. Pete bares his soul in this story, showing the courage to talk not only about his accomplishments, but also about his missteps and down-times. As I have mentioned, Pete's willingness to "tell it like it is", even when describing personal experiences that are not easy to talk about, is one of the qualities that caused me to like him from the start. Pete Shubin named his business *Goodguys*. What an appropriate name for a business built by a person who really is a *good guy!*

I appreciate how Pete has taken the time to write about his journey, his passion for his family, what he has learned about life and business, and how he became at one time the largest independent tire dealer from Bakersfield to Sacramento. He was born in a bathhouse on a farm in Iran, and left that village as a child in a horse-drawn wagon. How he came to be where he is and who he is today really is an amazing and worthwhile story to read and to learn from.

John Gamauf,
Former President of Bridgestone/Firestone North American Tire, Creator of BFNAT's Affiliated Dealer Program, and 2011 Inductee into the Tire Industry Hall of Fame.

PREFACE

I came to this country as a first-generation immigrant with nothing but the clothes on my back and whatever my mother could fit into a chest for our family of eight. We had left our village in Iran on a horse-drawn wagon, and after coming to America I worked as a field laborer from the time I was seven. In Kerman, Madera, San Jose, and Oregon, I picked everything that could be grown in those areas. In 1964, I started my adult life with twenty dollars, and from there I built up an organization that exceeded $30 million in annual sales while employing 120 people.

I am not as smart as my success might lead people to believe. I have operated by a few basic principles: Honesty, sacrifice, integrity, accountability, and being fair to my employees. Over the years, many people have said to me, "Pete, you should write a book on your career and the success of your business." Of all the people who have told me this, what stands out most is the comment of a retired banker who lives next door. One day this neighbor said, "Pete, what you have accomplished is unbelievable." Those words on that day are what really sparked me to get started in writing about *My Life as I Remember It*.

My purpose in writing this book is two-fold. One is to leave some history of myself and my family for my children, grandchildren, and future generations. The other is to show, by my own life example, how this country gives a person the opportunity to do anything he or she wants, *if in fact* the person will sacrifice the time and the effort into doing that. After all my travels in the world, I do not believe there is any other country that provides such opportunity.

INTRODUCTION

When I stepped onto the shores of America at the age of six, I saw a civilization far more developed than I could have imagined in my home village in Iran. From New York we came to Los Angeles, where I struggled to get my mind around this new world with its customs, its language, and its rapid pace. After a year in Los Angeles, my family moved back to the country, to a farm in Fresno County. At home, life continued in the ways I had always known, milking our cow, making our own bread, speaking our old language. Outside of my home, I had to learn what no school could have taught or prepared me for. Life in a new world. I cried a lot, because that was the only language I knew for expressing the experience of intimidation, of sometimes feeling overwhelmed, by the newness and sophistication of modern life. I think this experience is similar to what people can feel when stepping onto the road of entrepreneurship.

Among other reasons, I have written my story to help readers know that you can successfully navigate the risks and complexities of the business world by holding to a few basic principles, and, from there, by staying the course and remaining alert to what can be learned. The early chapters give some personal background, to show I was not born with a silver spoon in my mouth, and how the experiences of early life helped to develop in me certain character traits, such as sensitivity toward others, that have served me well in the responsibilities of leadership. The early history also shows how I started my way in business without having been formally educated in any of the areas I would eventually specialize in. This is important, because many have entered the competitive world of business loaded up with formal credentials, only to end up with an unexciting job that provides little opportunity for the full exercise of their talent and ambition.

In chapter seven, titled *Career Momentum*, I describe my start with Firestone under a store manager named Neil Sissleman, whose example in running a business did a lot to shape my understanding of how to put together and manage a business team. From there, I give entire chapters to detailed descriptions of how I built businesses in various industries, but mainly in tire and auto-repair. I talk about my missteps and how I learned from them, because I believe an entreprenuer's missteps can, in most cases, become some of the most important learning experiences.

Along the way, I do talk a lot about life outside of work, since my main motivation in writing this story is to perserve family history for the learning and enjoyment of my descendants and the Shubin generations to come. I want them to know me, not just as the builder of businesses, but as a son, brother, husband, uncle, father and step-father who loved his family and lived a full life. For the general reader, these portions of the book may not be interesting or useful, but they are important for my family's history.

I knew at an early age that I wanted to start my own business, rather than lock into a job where I could not explore and experiment as seemed best to me. Admittedly, that kind of a job carries less risk, whereas creating one's own business involves a lot more of the unknown and the unexpected. But for readers with an entrepreneurial impulse, I believe my story has a lot to contribute. You will read how I needed to make snap decisions on when to play it safe, and when to roll the dice. Discerning a good deal from a bad one involves more than just being smart. There is also an instinct that grows with time and experience for those who stay alert. Some of the qualities and principles that lead to success are not easily defined, but are better demonstrated through stories. I think my story presents, at least in some measure, these qualities and principles. I do not *guarantee* success to anyone, but I believe that reading my book will better position you for making effective decisions in the fast-paced and complex world of business.

CHAPTER ONE
WELCOME TO AMERICA!

On the ship to America!

From our slowly swaying ship I stared wide-eyed at a large green image as I heard someone say, "That is the Statue of Liberty." The date was May 21, 1951, a month shy of my sixth birthday. My parents and I, with my four brothers and younger sister, had set out from our small village of Rahmatabad, Iran, in a horse-drawn wagon with nothing but a few household belongings. My memories of the old country have long since faded, and my remembrance of life begins on the decks of that ship in New York Harbor.

Leaving home

In Rahmatabad, we had no hospitals or documents like birth certificates, but according to Mother's records kept in the family Bible, I was born in a steam bath (a BANA, the most sanitary place to give birth) on June 21st, 1945.

Our home in Rahmatabad, Iran

After that, for nearly six years I was raised on my father's tobacco farm, with the daily sights of horses, wagons, and familiar faces. In 1951, that was all replaced by an environment I would not have known how to imagine.

We had left Iran with eight other Russian families over Stalin's pressure on the Shah to return the older men of those households to Russia. Those men, all members of the pacifist Molokan religion, would certainly have been executed for not supporting either communism or Stalin's expansionist war efforts. For my father's part, he had escaped from a prison labor camp in 1933, leaving all of his hard-earned possessions behind as he fled in the night with my mother and two-year-old sister, Vera.

Shah of Iran talking with Pete's father and other village elders (c. 1950)

After their flight to Iran, for eighteen years my parents worked hard to purchase land, start a small business and raise a family, only to be forced once again to leave all possessions behind—house, farm, horses, wagons—in a flight for survival. As my father says in his memoirs: *In our life it seemed we always lived in a state of fleeing...relocating (p. 89)*. Even the money my parents had saved all went to government crooks in Tehran, as Father describes it: *We arrived in Tehran...we were Persian citizens. This citizenship was hard to take off, it cost a lot of money because there was a big bribe, like there was in Russia after the revolution. There was no set price, they just charged whatever they wanted...By the time they removed the citizenship we were totally wrung out...[Relatives in the U.S.] sent us $1,000, they had taken up a collection in America from people here and there (p. 60)*. After so much hard work and all that my parents had already been through in life, they now stood penniless in the harbor of a country whose language they did not know.

My first sight in America!

Crossing the Atlantic, Mother suffered severe seasickness and was hospitalized in the large ship's infirmary, but she was a strong woman and helped my father lead us off the ship with a firm hand. I remember seeing what I think was the Brooklyn Bridge, feeling amazed at the sight of so many cars. From there, we found temporary lodging through the support of relatives who had come to America ahead of us, including Vera, now twenty and living in Los Angeles with her husband, John Volkoff. John's family shared a deep history with my family, going back to the times and the hardships in Russia. After two days we were taxied to a bus station where we boarded a Greyhound for our cross-country trip to California on the old Route 66.

Riding the Greyhound was an experience in itself, so different from the wagons and rickety roads we were accustomed to. The bus was crowded, mostly with Russians from our group of families, and according to Father's memoirs, *we traveled four days on the Greyhound…hungry, cold, and sleep deprived (p. 74).* But what stands out most in my memory are the parades and other festivities we saw from the bus windows in each little town we passed through. America was celebrating Memorial Day Weekend, but we did not know anything about that. One of my cousins knew a bit of English, and he asked the driver what these American people were so happy about? The driver told him, "They are celebrating you guys coming to America!" When I heard this through the translator, I felt pretty good! To think the people of America would care about us and be happy that we had come to live in their country! We passed through many small and mid-sized towns on that long journey, and then we came to the tall buildings and maze of roads in Los Angeles.

CHAPTER TWO
LOS ANGELES

At the Greyhound Bus Terminal in Los Angeles, John Volkoff and Vera helped to gather our luggage and then drove us to their home in Maywood, not in a wagon but in a car! I remember standing by their front yard and watching water spray out of little gadgets in the ground. "What are those?", I asked someone in Russian. "Those are sprinklers," the person answered. After it was explained to me what sprinklers are and what they do, I felt amazed. Then they took us around to the back and showed us a small house with two bedrooms. This would be our new home.

We arrived about the time summer vacation was starting, so when we went out of the house to explore the neighborhood, we saw kids everywhere. We became immediate targets because of our handmade clothing and because we could not understand the language. The second or third time we went out, the other kids attacked us with squirt guns. We ran back inside to grab ours, but it was the only one we had. We were hopelessly outgunned, especially since one of the neighborhood kids had a bazooka squirter, a prized weapon among the kids of L.A. in those days. It was the Shubins against the neighborhood! After being ruthlessly drenched, my brother Bill, the oldest among the boys, ran inside and filled our squirter with pepper juice. When he came back out, the other kids rushed toward him, but instead of trying to cover himself, Bill boldly stepped forward and started squirting at their faces. Boy did those kids hightail it, like yelping dogs with their tails between their legs.

My parents had to find work as soon as possible, not only to provide for our family but also to repay what they had borrowed for the journey. Finding work was not easy, as Father explains in his memoirs: *We needed to provide for our families [and] we wanted to pay our debts...I went here and I went there looking for work. I could not find work...When I walked down the road people stared at me because I did not even know what the signs meant...When it said, 'STOP', we would walk, people would holler and laugh* (p. 75). Father added that when he did find work, his boss would say, *'Bring me a hammer,' and I would bring a shovel. I did everything opposite because I did not understand the language (p. 76)*. Eventually, Father got a job in a factory making $1.25 an hour, and Mom went to work doing piecework, sewing up holes in gunny sacks and things like that. They had to work full time while trying to raise a young daughter and five boys running around like wild Indians. How they made it, I do not know, except that my parents had learned to survive and succeed in any circumstances, and to continue living with principle and determination.

Some of the neighborhood kids had swimming pools in their family homes, but we were never invited for a swim. One blazing summer day we were talking about how much we would like to have our own pool, and brother Bill came up with the idea of creating one in the cellar of our house. We cleaned it up and put a water hose in it, and we really had a blast splashing around in that makeshift pool, but when Mom and Dad came home and saw what we had done to the cellar, boy did they beat our butts!

When the school year started in September of 1951, although I was six years old, they put me in kindergarten. Well, we had a neighbor girl named Hazel, about ten years old, and Hazel loved to roller skate. On school days she would hold my hand as we skated to our school about two blocks away. Hazel would walk me to my class, and as soon as she left, I would start crying. In those days, you could look at me sideways and I would cry. I could not tell people how I felt or what I wanted to say. The teacher did not understand me, and I did not understand her, and none of the kids in the class could interpret. So, without exaggeration, the only memory I have of my kindergarten classroom is of me sitting at my desk and crying. After a while, the teacher hit on the strategy of letting me go out and play in the sandbox where I would not cry. So instead of sitting in class with the rest of the kids, I got to go out and play in the sandbox!

Not long after school let out in summer of 1952, someone told my dad, "Why don't you take your kids up to Kerman for the grape harvest? You can do pretty well with your boys working with you." So, leaving Mother and little sister at home, Dad packed us up in a 1937 Pontiac and we headed north for a 220-mile drive.

1937 Pontiac

Now, the roads back then were not like today. It was anything but a straight drive from L.A. to the Fresno area, and Father could not read or speak English. How he got us there, I do not know, but it was not the first time he had to find his way along in a difficult situation. In 1933, after escaping from the Soviet work camp, Father led Mother and Vera through the mountains from Turkmenistan to Iran while dodging Stalin's deadly police. In fact, I would like to relate a little more of that history here, since it is not only interesting but also shows how people can succeed by putting their backbone into life, even when the cards are stacked against them.

The communists had taken everything my father owned, as he says in his memoirs: *They confiscated all the houses, horses, wagons, big items, and let us keep the household belongings only* (p. 22) He was sent to a labor camp with brutally harsh conditions, working daily with the same hunger that drove a lot of the men to eat turtle soup for survival. Many died, and had Father stayed in those conditions he also would likely have perished. Determined to not give up on life, he formed a plan to escape and take his small family to Iran.

Father somehow communicated the plan to Mother, and with help from a relative he obtained train tickets. On the appointed night he slipped out of the camp and met Mother and two-year-old Vera near a train station. Obviously, if he had been spotted by anyone in Stalin's massive police force, they would have arrested and swiftly executed him. The three of them boarded the train, and for several days they rode in fear of being noticed by police or informants. Father talks in his memoirs about fearing that Stalin's officials *will hold us up at the next train station and detain us, or possibly the next one. But we passed one station after another and nobody detained us.* (p. 24)

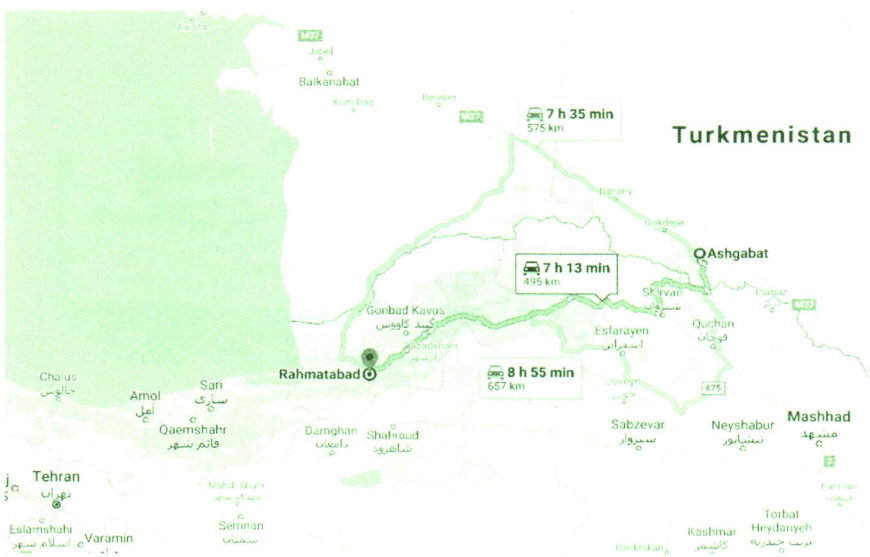

My father's escape route. Map courtesy of Google Maps.

Mother and Vera (c. 1933)

Type of train used in Father's escape from Russia

Their plan was to jump off as near to the Persian border as possible. In a mountainous region in Turkmenistan, about forty-five miles from the border, as they saw a curve coming up in the tracks, Mother tied Vera to Father's back, and they all jumped. After hitting the ground, they tumbled and rolled, and somehow Father kept Vera from harm while he and Mother suffered only scrapes and light bruises. Then, traveling at night for fear of being spotted, the only landmarks Father had were the angle of the setting sun and the position of the stars. Night after night he led the journey with little food and little water, until they reached the border and crossed into Iran where I was born.

With that kind of navigation experience under his belt, it does not surprise me that Father got us from Los Angeles to Kerman over a maze of unknown roads without being able to read or speak a lick of English. We arrived in Kerman on August 24 and spent the rest of summer vacation picking grapes. It was very dirty work, and in those days they did not spray for wasps, so each time I stuck my face in a grapevine I knew there could be a swarm waiting to rush out after me. I could not count how many times I got stung, but for me that was just a fact of life.

A typical workday involved getting up early and having breakfast, working till ten and stopping for a snack, and then back to work till lunch. After that, we took a thirty-minute nap, then got back to work till sundown and went home for dinner. Sometimes I would see other kids playing baseball or riding bicycles, and of course I wished I could do that instead of working all day, but I was with my family and we were together, so I was not unhappy.

With his boys helping, by the end of harvest Father had made $630, more American money than he had ever seen. Because of our work ethic, we were asked to stay two more weeks to turn and roll trays, which was back-breaking work where we were literally bent over for a quarter of a mile at a time with dust and sand in our faces, in temperatures over a hundred degrees. That was tough work, but for our labor Dad made an additional three hundred and sixty dollars!

Father sent word to Mother that there seemed no sense in staying in Los Angeles, because with all of the boys working, the family could earn far more money in the Fresno area. Mother was only a couple months away from giving birth to my youngest sister, Annie, but next thing we knew, she came to Kerman and we settled in for our career in farming.

CHAPTER THREE
GROWING UP ON A FARM

House on Trinity Ave., Kerman CA. Still standing!

We moved into a shabby, two-bedroom house out in the country on Trinity Avenue, with five boys in one room and everyone else in the other. (That old house from the 1950s is still standing.) On the night of December 17, 1952, Mother gave birth to Annie. Kerman was covered by a thick fog, and visibility was so bad that the doctor would not drive out to our house. A midwife helped to deliver Annie, and two more days passed before the fog cleared and the doctor came out to check on Mom and sign the birth certificate. In Russia and Iran, Mother had given birth to all her children at home, and she did the same in America.

I started the first grade at Empire Elementary School in Kerman. My English by this time was fairly good, and

Bill, Alex, Jim, Pete, Michael, Linda, Annie (c. 1953)

there were some Russian kids in my class who helped with the language when I still needed that. At home we spoke Russian but outside the house it was English, and we were expected to do good in both languages. I was starting to feel more comfortable as an American. When we had first come to the U.S., Mother made all our clothes, and along with the language issue, this made us stand out everywhere as immigrants. But by the time I started the second grade, we were earning enough income for Father to buy us store-bought clothes.

Although the school year had begun, we still needed to work, getting up early for a couple hours in the fields, then back to work after school, as well as from sun-up till sundown on Saturdays. Sunday was church day and doing chores around the house. That is how it went, year after year. At home we milked our own cow, made our own cheese, baked our own bread and butchered our own beef. When school was let out each year, instead of enjoying a summer vacation playing with other kids in the neighborhood, we first went to San Jose where we picked and cut apricots, and after the apricots, we picked prunes. Then, when the work was finished in San Jose, Dad packed us into the truck and we went to Woodburn, Oregon, to pick strawberries, loganberries and string beans. I hated picking the string beans because garden snakes would hide in the vines, and we never knew when we might have a snake in our hand. Then, about the time the string bean season was finishing in Oregon, the grape harvest was starting again in Kerman. Since that harvest went on past the end of summer vacation, every year we missed the first week or two of school.

In the places where we worked, the farmers were always good to us because they wanted us to come back the following year. We slept on boxes in their barns or whatever living quarters they had for us. Father took us often to a public swimming pool and told us to enjoy a swim, but we knew the real reason was for us to take a bath!

We also made good money picking cotton. We got paid four cents a pound, and each of us could pick about 200 pounds on a good day. As we picked the cotton, we had to stuff it in large sacks, about ten or twelve feet long, and it was back-breaking work. Then we had to climb a ladder with our sacks, cross a narrow board laid across a trailer, and dump the cotton out of the sack. We picked cotton till dark, and sometimes it got hard to see the scales where we had to weigh the bags before dumping them. I remember one night when we were using matches to see the scales, and brother Alex noticed the end of a piece of cotton sticking through the chicken wire of the trailer. Well, he thought it would be a good idea to burn off that piece of cotton because it just did not look right sticking out like that. Brother Jim and I were *inside* the trailer packing it, and when brother Alex put a match to that piece of cotton, the whole trailer lit up in a flash! Somehow Jim and I jumped out in time, so we did not get burned, but that trailer smoked for months from the smoldering cotton seeds. If I remember right, Father had to pay whatever the farmer's insurance did not cover.

To help motivate us, my parents competed us boys with each other, sort of like racehorses. They would say something like, "Hey, Pete, brother Jim has more trays than you." Or, "Hey, Pete, you're working too slow, look at how much more brother Alex has." We were raised to be very competitive, and we would fight a lot with each other, but if anyone else tried to start a problem with one of us, the other four were ready to jump in. Life went on this way, and although I hated the constant work, I was not unhappy. It was all I knew, and I accepted it without question.

Year after year we helped Father earn a good income, and by 1955 he had saved enough to buy *with cash* a 20-acre farm in Kerman. This was only four years after coming to America penniless and in debt.

In 1957 I started the sixth grade, and for the first time I had a male teacher. His name was Mr. McFall, and I remember him bringing in model airplanes, the kind that fly. During recess, Mr. McFall would put those roaring planes up in the air with all of us kids watching. Well, one day a plane got away and fell somewhere in a vineyard, so we all ran out to search but nobody could find it. The vineyard was in an area between our home and the school, and one day a few months later as I passed through that vineyard, I spotted the plane! I brought it to Mr. McFall, and he made me feel like a great hero. Also, sometimes he would let us boys put on boxing gloves and have matches with one-minute rounds. I remember winning a match against a kid named Jimmy Montagu. Those are fun memories from my early school years.

Me at age 8

Title Deed to Kerman Farm, 1955

I was a fairly good baseball player, and of course I never got to play Little League because we had to work, but sometimes at school we had softball games and I loved them. One day when I was in the 6th grade, and my brother Jim was in the 7th, somebody organized a game between my class and his. Now, remember that my brothers and I were very competitive with each other, so in the days leading up to the game there was a lot of excitement in our home and at our school, and even more so because our older brother Alex was going to be the umpire! The day came, and the game went down to the last inning, with me on third base and the score tied. Jim, who was playing catcher, somehow missed a pitched ball, so I took off for home. It was a close call, but I beat Jim to the plate and our brother Alex was there to call me "Safe!" Boy was Jim mad at me!

In those days, Mother still baked our bread and made each of us a sandwich for school, while the other kids ate cafeteria food. It was comical because the kids at school were eyeing my homemade bread, while I was eyeing their cafeteria sandwiches. One day I made a deal with a friend named Lee Nielmier, and we started swapping sandwiches until the teacher got word of it.

Advancing from the sixth to the seventh grades was interesting. In Kerman, the Junior-High and the High School were on the same campus and in the same buildings. The seventh graders were so much smaller than the kids in the higher grades, and they called us "scroungees." For example, the campus had a snack bar that was very popular with the students, but it was only for the high schoolers. If one of us kids from the 7th or 8th grades tried to buy anything, the older students would say, "You're a scroungee! You can't buy anything here."

Overall, I had a good time in my Junior-High years, except for the occasions when I was sent to see Mr. Echols, the school principal. In those days, teachers could keep the kids in line by whacking their butts with a paddle, and Mr. Echols kept in his office a wooden paddle with holes drilled in it. When he swung it, the wind came right through those holes, and boy could you feel it when that paddle landed! I was sent to see him more than once, but never for anything extremely serious. Also, in Junior High I tried learning how to play the Saxophone, but I did not have the time to learn how to read music, and I could not get the hang of how to blow properly into the instrument. That basically ended my experiment in music.

About the time I became a teenager, I began feeling uncomfortable with the Molokans. To help explain this, let me give some background. When the Russian Molokans migrated from Russia, a lot of them came directly to the U.S., before and during the Stalin era. A lot of them also went to Mexico and Brazil, whereas we were among those who went to Iran. When we got to the Fresno area, the other kids in the Molokan church would call us "Persians", which in that context was a very derogatory expression. By my teenage years I was feeling more and more comfortable identifying with the wider community, rather than with the Molokans. Over time, that distance only grew.

In 1959, Father was able to buy a 100-acre farm in Madera, on Avenue 17 and Highway 99, about thirty miles from our land in Kerman. He now owned two farms totaling 120 acres! But owning two farms meant *working* two farms, so Dad purchased a brand-new Massey Ferguson 50 tractor, which was actually very small for that much land. We hauled it between farms using shabby equipment for the transport. Looking back, we were lucky none of us got hurt. The Madera farm was hard land to work, as it was not level, and this made irrigation difficult. The property had a lot of hardpan in some places and was very sandy in others. I think the only reason Father bought it is because he got it for a low price.

Buying the land in Madera meant that we needed to relocate, so Father and Mother decided to build a new house on the farm. This also meant that I had to transfer schools and start the tenth grade at Madera High. That was my first experience with racial segregation, and overall, the school was a cultural shock to me. I had to make new friends, but the most challenging thing was finding time to focus enough on my schoolwork to get passing grades, since I had to work hours each weekday before and after school, and all day on Saturdays. I managed to pass all my classes, although I barely squeaked out with a D-minus in Algebra and another one in Spanish. Those teachers agreed to pass me only if I promised to check out of their classes!

CHAPTER FOUR
DRIFTING FROM MY ROOTS

In the eleventh grade I started hanging out with friends who liked to smoke and drink. I never took up smoking, but I did take to drinking, and we had a local liquor store that would sell alcohol to just about anybody. One Monday morning in school, after I had partied most of the night before, I could not dress out for P.E. because I was too hung over. My P.E. teacher saw me laying on the ground and he said, "There's nothing wrong with you, except that you drank all night!" Then he stepped on my stomach and I almost threw up. That is one example of how the drinking was affecting my life in a negative way, and I could have been a much better student had I stayed away from the bad friends and the alcohol. But I also made some good friends, and I have a lot of positive memories from those times, like in wood shop when I made a beautiful cedar chest for my mother, which I still have, and also one for my sister-in-law, Martha.

In the summer between my Junior and Senior years (1963), my parents bought me a 1955 Chevy two-door hardtop with a wonder bar radio and a floor shift converted from a column shift. The car had a 265 cubic inch engine bored to make it a 283. It had a race cam and solid lifters, and because of its rough idle I named it *The Percolator*. A friend named Neil Averil pinstriped it and painted

The Percolator on both rear fenders with fancy lettering. I thought I was hot stuff because not too many kids had cars, but what the other kids did not know is that my parents bought it so I could get home sooner after school to work on the farm!

My senior year was fun because I had the car and I could take it into auto shop and work on it. I was also the foreman in wood shop, but since the classes were next to each other I would take roll call and then disappear from wood shop to work on my car in auto. The love of cars and working on cars was growing in me, and ever since the days of auto shop and *The Percolator*, one thing that has always been important to me is having a nice car.

Reproduction of The Percolator!

The cedar chest I made for mother

During my senior year I was doing a lot of party-drinking and dating non-Russian girls. One night during a party out in the country, a friend of my brother Jim's was driving my car because I had too much to drink. As we barreled down a road, I saw one of the local constables, Gene Petrocelli, coming our way. I said to the driver, "Heck, just run him off the road." So, he did it! He drove old Gene right off the road.

Wouldn't you know it, two Highway Patrolmen saw all of this and pulled us over. When one of the officers came to the passenger side and asked for my identification, I handed him an empty wallet and purposely dropped it. As he leaned down to pick up the wallet I took off, running like a jackrabbit through the nearest grape field. The officer chased me but could not catch me, and I am lucky he did not shoot me! Somewhere out in that field I laid down and fell asleep until five in the morning. Jim's friend went to jail, and my car got towed.

I mentioned the local constable, Gene, but I would like to say a little more about him. Gene had a sidekick named Hiney Wolfe. Back then, we did not have a Sheriff's Department, so Gene and Hiney were like County Mounties, deputized to watch the whole county. One thing I remember about Gene is how he carried an illegal, sawed-off shotgun, and whenever they pulled us over and found beer, Gene would set our beer bottles on grape posts and use them for target practice. We used to get so mad, just standing there watching him have a good time shooting up our beer!

Gene and Hiney knew all of us Russian kids, and they were always pulling us over and shaking us down for alcohol. They never took any of us to jail, mainly because the nearest jail was thirty-five miles away! They would just lecture us and send us home.

Sometimes our episodes with Gene and Hiney resembled scenes from a later show, The Dukes of Hazzard, like the time we stole some of those blinking lights used for warning drivers about a flooded area. In those days, when the kids had parties out in the country near Kerman, they would grab some of those lights from a roadside and throw them in the back of their truck. Then they drove to some area where they wanted to have a party, and they set up the lights to make other drivers think the road was closed, when actually the kids were using that stretch of road to have a street party. Well, one night a friend and I were out driving in a truck and we saw a couple of those lights, so we stopped and threw them in the back of our truck. We were coming from Madera, which is right over the river from Kerman, and about a quarter mile from the river we saw Hiney coming toward us in the opposite direction. I watched his face as he passed, staring at those blinking lights with a look that said, "What the heck!" He did a screeching U-Turn and started chasing us, so we stopped at a place by the river and quickly threw the lights in the water, thinking they would sink. But instead of sinking, the lights went floating down the river, blinking in the dark.

By the time Hiney caught up to us, the lights were out of sight. He hopped out of his car and stood in front of us, looking around and wondering what happened to those lights. Finally, he said, "I saw those blinking lights, now where did you put 'em?" We did a good job of playing stupid, and of course he knew we had done something with them, but they were nowhere to be seen so he had nothing to work with. He just shook his head, then searched us to see if we had any beer he could confiscate, and when he could not find anything, he sent us on our way.

Well, about thirty years later, when my youngest son Danny was going to school in Clovis, one of his teachers was Hiney Wolfe's son, Ken. My son used to playfully tell Ken, "This is what my dad did to your dad," so the younger Wolfe knew all about that little story with the lights. On Danny's graduation day, he came up to me and said, "Hey Dad, I want to introduce you to somebody." I followed him, and when he had brought me to an elderly man, he said, "Do you know who this is?" I looked at the older fellow and said, "No." Danny smiled and said, "This is Hiney Wolfe!" When Hiney realized who I was, before I could say anything, he pointed his finger at me and said, "I *knew* you boys were guilty. I should've hauled you in!" Boy did we get a laugh out of that.

In my later high school years, I increasingly drifted from the strict community which my parents regarded as "our people." After graduating, in 1964, my parents sent me to Los Angeles to live with brother Alex and his wife, who were very strict Molokans. I think my parents were hoping that in L.A. I might re-connect with "our people" and merge my life back into the Molokan culture and community. Father gave me $20 and a full tank of gas, and Mother gave me a pillow and a blanket. Before leaving Fresno, I drove by to see my brother-in-law, John Volkoff (they had moved to the Fresno area), and asked if I could borrow some money, pointing out that $20 was not going to get me very far. John answered that if Father wanted me to have more money, he would have given it to me. So, on the morning of June 14th, I drove away from Madera in *The Percolator* and went out into the world.

CHAPTER FIVE
OUT ON MY OWN

Me at age eighteen

During the drive to Los Angeles, a million things were going through my mind. There was no plan to follow, no savings to draw from, and no group of old friends to hang out with. For the first time in my life, I was on my own. The tank of gas got me to the bottom of the Grapevine, and after stopping at a station and filling the tank, *The Percolator* would not start. I asked the attendant for a jump, and he said yes, but that it would cost me five dollars! So, after the refueling, the jump start, and buying a Coke, I had eight dollars left to start my career.

Alex and his wife let me live in a one-bedroom apartment behind their garage. They charged me $100 a month and laid down a lot of rules: I could not party, I had to be home by ten at night, and I could not have friends at the apartment. The next day I went out job-hunting, and I was hired by a company called L.A. News, sort of the old version of Office Depot. I filled orders in a warehouse, and my take-home pay was about $48 a week. As you can see, my room and board were costing me half my monthly income. After about three months, brother Alex asked me to leave, so I moved in with brother Bill and his wife, Martha. Both of them are Molokans, but they did not put on me all the same rules as brother Alex.

While living with Bill I started two new jobs, one in the daytime hours at Kern's Fine Foods where I canned juices, and one in the night hours pumping gas at a Mobil station on Atlantic Blvd. and Montebello Street. Looking back, this is where my career really started. The owner hired me as an attendant (gassing up cars, cleaning windshields, etc.), but there was a lot of down time on the gas island, so I was able to spend hours hanging out with the mechanic in the garage. After the mechanic saw my interest and how fast I picked up on things, he started letting me do oil changes. After a while, he began teaching me how to do brake jobs, which I already knew from auto shop, but he had a different way of doing things.

During that time, the military tried to draft me, but because of color-blindness I was exempted from service. That freed me to focus on learning about the auto-service industry. Since I enjoyed working on cars and was good at it, by this time I knew my career would be in tire and auto-repair.

After a year at Mobil, I applied for a job at Firestone as a brake and front-end mechanic. A district supervisor named Ed Gornack interviewed me, and although I knew very little about front-end work or using the equipment for that work, I presented myself as knowing what I was talking about. For all of my references, I put places that had gone out of business and could not be checked. After the interview, Gornack said he would check my references and call me back. Evidently, he did not check anything, because one week later he called and asked if I had the tools to do the job. I assured him I did, even though I did not have any of the tools and knew very little about the kind of work I was being hired to do! When I told brother Bill about the situation, he let me use his Sears credit card to go and buy the biggest tool chest they had and fill it with tools. Then I spent the weekend getting the tools dirty and looking worn, so they would seem used and I would seem qualified for the job.

I reported to work at the Firestone store in Glendale, where the head mechanic, Bob, quickly saw that I did not have much experience in front-end work or alignments. On the second day, I admitted this to Bob, and I asked him for help. He said yes, but that in two weeks he was transferring to Dallas, meaning I would need to learn quickly because in ten days I would be the head mechanic at the Glendale Firestone store! Well, since the store manager and sales people knew nothing about brake and front-end work, and since they rarely came into the shop (they gave the impression that even the chance of getting dirty was beneath them), they assumed I was an expert. When someone did try to question me on work that I did not yet know how to do very well, I responded with an attitude, saying something like, "You want to come over here and do it yourself?" That approach worked well as a cover-up for the fact that I was not nearly as experienced as they thought!

Of course, I could not possibly learn all that was needed in only two weeks, but just as Bob was leaving for Dallas, Firestone hired a mechanic named Marvin as an assistant to me. Marvin was a former linebacker for the Chicago Bears, and his football career had ended with a leg injury that left him walking with a limp. He was at least ten years older than me, and he helped a lot with my hot-headed attitude, as well as with getting the work done. Between the two of us we did a great job, and no one else ever knew I had started that position with almost no knowledge of how to do the work I was hired for.

Working at the Glendale store for Firestone was a good job that paid good money, but after two years I quit because of the way Ed Gornack treated his employees. What brought it to a head was when he ordered everyone to stay for overtime until the store met its quota for the day. He warned that anyone who left would be fired, so I locked up my toolbox and went home, considering myself fired. The next day I came by to pick up my tools, and when the store manager, Phil Graham, told me I was not really fired, I told him I did not want to continue working there. I left Firestone and applied for a job at Uniroyal. Since I now had experience and could speak like an industry veteran, they hired me the next day.

CHAPTER SIX
FALLING IN LOVE

Reneé at age eighteen   Me at age 22

One Saturday night in early 1966 I went to a Russian party and saw a beautiful girl whom I wanted to approach but was too drunk to try. Well, the very next day at a reception after a wedding, the same girl was there. I built up enough courage to ask her to dance, and her eager response indicated she had been hoping I would ask! She told me her name was Reneé Shubin, and after telling her we have the same last name, I asked where she was from. She said, "I'm from San Francisco." Well, I knew all the Russian girls from that city and had never heard of a Reneé Shubin, so I was curious about all of this. After a couple of dances,

I asked if she would like to go out for a burger and a coke. She agreed, and off we went.

Reneé and I were enjoying our time together, and as the conversation warmed up, she told me she was not really a Russian, and that she was not really from San Francisco but lived in the Fresno area. The girls who had accompanied her to Los Angeles for the wedding told her that only Russians would be welcomed in the church. They advised her that if anyone asks about her last name, to tell them she is a Shubin, a common last name in the Russian community, and that she lives in San Francisco. Reneé seemed a bit nervous as she told me this, naturally wondering what my response would be. I laughed and told her something like, "You don't know how relieved I am! Let me tell you, I've had really bad luck with Russian girls." We both had a good laugh about that, and things warmed up all the more between us.

Reneé and I began dating, with me making a weekly drive from L.A. to Fresno and going through a lot of money to pay for those trips. I started using a Union Oil credit card, and after running up a nice little debt, I quit making payments. Well, of course they wanted their money, so they started looking for me, but I kept changing addresses and they were not able to catch up. I thought it was funny about buying all that gas without paying for it, and that was just one example of my irresponsible attitude in those days.

Reneé was a Junior in high school when we started dating, so we had to wait for her to graduate before she could join me in Los Angeles. We dated secretly so that my parents would not know I was in love with a non-Russian. But she and my sister were in the same grade and went to the same school, so when I drove up to Kerman and accompanied Reneé to the Junior Prom, my sister got word of it. That was how my family found out I was dating a non-Russian!

After a couple years I tried introducing Reneé to my parents, but they would not have anything to do with her. One of my brothers told me that if I married without our parents' consent, I would be guilty of adultery and would go to hell! I dismissed this as ridiculous, but it was very painful to hear such things and to have my fiancée rejected by my family.

Me and Reneé, July 20, 1968

We set the wedding for July 20th in Carmel, and we sent out invitations to everyone. All of Reneé's family members came, but not one came from mine. This was very heartbreaking, and the silent treatment from my family went on for about a year.

Reneé was a very warm-hearted person who made friends easily. I was happy with her, and for about three years we enjoyed our life together while living in a small apartment in the city of Bell. But I still had a lot of bad habits that needed to be broke.

One of my bad habits from those days was going to a bar to shoot some pool and have a couple cold ones after work, sometimes not getting home until very late. Also, I was addicted to gambling and often got together with friends in the back of a liquor store in Pico Rivera, where the card games could last until 3:00 in the morning (even when I had to be at work a few hours later). On one occasion, I came home drunk at about 10:00, and Reneé told me she was leaving. I said, "I'm going with you," and she said, "Fine." As she was heading out to her car, I quickly put on a pair of shorts and cowboy boots, but no shirt. I jumped in the car just as she was taking off, and after a couple minutes I said to her, "I don't like the way you're driving." She said, "Would you like to drive?" I said, "Yes." We were in Lynwood, a short distance from Watts, hardly the best place for me to be out on the streets at that time of night!

Reneé pulled over somewhere near an intersection, but when I got out to come around to the driver's side, she took off! I stood there in my shorts and boots, thinking she would come back, but she just kept going. For the first time in my life, I started to hitch-hike. A few minutes later I got picked up by a guy who seemed that he had more in mind than just giving me a ride home. At a red light not far from my apartment, I jumped out, thanked him, and walked the rest of the way.

Another example of my youthful arrogance was that I did not pay the fines on my traffic tickets. I thought this was funny, until one night I got picked up on a warrant and brother Bill had to come and bail me out!

I had to appear in a courthouse in Compton on one of those violations, and the judge I stood before had a nickname, "The Laughing Judge of Compton." He had earned that name because of the times he listened to a plea, made a joke out of it, and then dismissed the case while telling the person not to come back. On that particular day he had not fined anyone, so when my turn came, I expected a break. He said to me, "How do you plead?" I told him, "Guilty, your Honor, with an excuse." He said, "What's your excuse?" I told him I had recently gotten married and spent all my money on the honeymoon, so I could not afford the fine. At that point Reneé and I were the only ones left in the courtroom. The judge looked over at her and said, "Is that the lady you married?" I said, "Yes, your Honor." He said, "Why would such a beautiful lady marry someone who can't pay a traffic ticket?" I looked up at him and said, "Because I'm good looking, your Honor." Well, I do not think he liked that answer. He said to me, "Okay, good looking, it's either a one-hundred dollar fine or three days in jail." I chose the fine (he gave me ninety days to pay it), and that was the only fine he gave for that whole day. Boy, did Reneé ever tease me about that one.

A little more than a year after the wedding, my parents stopped by at our apartment in Bell, telling us they would like to bless our marriage with a Russian minister at their home in Kerman. We agreed, and a month later we drove up to Kerman where all of my family members attended the ceremony and wanted to be friends with Reneé! I was grateful for that, but for some time it was still difficult to forget how we were treated.

CHAPTER SEVEN
CAREER MOMENTUM

In 1968, I was personally recruited by a Firestone district manager to come on board as a mechanic at a store in North Hollywood. His name was Neil Sissleman, and the store was about six months away from completion. Neil had asked Firestone to demote him to the position of store manager so he could fulfill his dream of running a location with a handpicked team. I accepted the job, and Neil became a mentor to me. Everything I learned from him, I went on to use throughout my long career in the tire and auto-repair business.

Neil built a crew that worked together, like a football team with each person having his own position. There was a playbook, there were monthly meetings and objectives for each department, there was a budget to meet each month, and the mechanics were treated the same as the salesmen. In most of the locations I had worked at, the employees in sales looked at us guys in the shop like we were nothing, and they seemed to feel it was beneath them to even spend time in the shop. When a consumer dropped off his or her car, the mechanics would look it over and tell the salesman what was needed, and typically the salesman would not even come out to the shop and look at the car. Neil changed all of that by requiring his salesmen to inspect the cars and make sure that what the mechanics were saying was factual, and also so the salesmen could actually know what they were talking about (since they were the ones who had to sell the job which the mechanics said was needed).

As I said, Neil built a team and worked his business around that team. He required accountability and professionalism from everyone, showed favoritism to no one, and earned strong respect from the people who worked for him. That is what I learned from watching how Neil Sissleman ran his store, and those policies have served me well in the years of running my own businesses. To this day, my store managers and salesmen are never going to sell anything to a consumer without going out and looking at the car to make sure that what the mechanic is saying is factual.

During that time of working in North Hollywood, a wonderful development took place in my life. On June 12th, 1970, my first son was born. We named him Scott Eric Shubin. Before Scott came into the world, I was real excited about having a baby, and in those days the doctors could not know whether the child was a boy or a girl. But Grandma knew an old trick, and one day she tied a pencil to a string and held it over Reneé's stomach. Grandma told us that if the pencil made big circles, the baby was a boy, and if it made small circles, it was a girl. Well, when Grandma applied the test, the pencil made big circles, so that is how we knew we were having a boy.

The day came when Reneé said to me, "It's time." I rushed her to the hospital and dropped her off at Emergency, where the attendants put her in a wheelchair while I went out to park the car. By the time I came back in, Scott was born. Five pounds and twelve ounces, at 8:57 in the morning. When I first looked at my son, I thought he was the most beautiful baby I had ever seen. For some reason, what stands out in my memory is how skinny his legs were. When Reneé's brother, Doug, came to our apartment to see the baby, he said, "He looks like a wharf rat!" I stood up and threw him out of our apartment, telling him, "If you can't come up with something better than that, then get out." Some people just have a problem with saying the wrong thing.

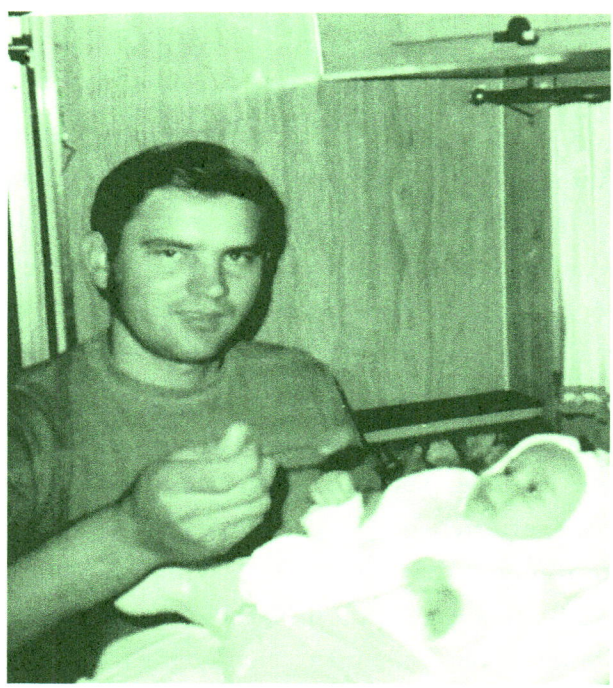

Me with Scott at our apartment in Bell

Reneé and I started our new adventure with three family members instead of two. Some of my memories of those early days with Scott are when we would take him out in his stroller every day after I came home from work. Sometimes we went to a nearby park about a half-mile from the apartment, where Scott would sit in his stroller while Reneé and I played badminton. I also remember how we would strap him in his little car seat and head off to Lake Elsinore to ski on the boat we purchased soon after he was born. Elsinore, out in Riverside County, was our favorite lake. We would put Scott in a little swing tied to a low-hanging branch, and it was so cute that sometimes I would just sit there and watch him. At Elsinore we liked to hit the water about six in the morning and ski until mid-day, then take a break to cook hamburgers or marinate steaks, and then go back out on the lake till after sundown. Those were really fun times.

Around Christmas of 1971, we went to Fresno to spend time with our families during the holidays, and we started talking about moving back there. My drive to work from Bell to North Hollywood was about an hour each way through busy traffic, but more importantly, Reneé and I did not want to raise Scott and our future kids in Los Angeles. Before leaving Fresno after the Holiday celebration, we purchased a three-bedroom house at 1206 W. Indianapolis Avenue, and we put it up for rent to make some extra income until we made our move back to the Fresno area.

When we returned to Los Angeles, I told Neil that I loved working for him, but that I would be leaving in a maximum of six months. Well, for those six months there was hardly a day when Neil did not try to persuade me to change my mind. As much as I respected him, I stayed with my decision. When I left for Fresno, in June of 1972, our store was the best-earning service store in Los Angeles, and my co-worker and I were the highest paid Firestone mechanics.

CHAPTER EIGHT
GETTING STARTED IN FRESNO

Shortly before moving, I sent out resumes to all the major tire dealers in the Fresno area. Firestone did not have any company-owned stores there, so I could not transfer. After moving, I got a response from B.F. Goodrich, and I went to see them. The interview was going well until they told me I would have to cut my hair. Although my hair was not really that long, I was not going to cut it for anyone, so I walked away from that opportunity. I also got responses from other companies, but I ended up choosing to work for Goodyear at their modern, ten bay facility in the Fulton Mall.

Goodyear had two different types of payrolls. One was for temporary workers who did not receive benefits because they were placed only on a local payroll and were not on the payroll at Goodyear's headquarters in Akron, Ohio. I told the store manager that I would not take the job unless they put me on the Akron payroll with commission pay and benefits from day one. The store management agreed to this, but somehow my paperwork got "lost" and I did not get a commission check for two months. One day I told them I would quit unless they paid me what I had coming. Management liked my work, so they stepped up for me and Akron instructed them to give me back-pay for those two months. They also agreed to pay me daily from the cash drawer until all the paperwork got straightened out, meaning that each day I went home with a wad of cash in my pocket in an area that was not very safe!

I quickly realized that the tire stores in Fresno did everything from the Stone Ages. For example, in Los Angeles a pair of mechanics was expected to do six to eight brake jobs a day plus the front-end work, just to show they were qualified. In Fresno it was not like that. The mechanics would milk one job for half a day, and smoke for the other half. A lot of things like that were going on. When I came to work at the Fulton Mall store, I applied my Los Angeles tactics and quickly started making much more bonus pay than the other two mechanics.

Instead of following the example of my work ethic, the other mechanics started complaining to the store manager, Glen Huntington, that my bonus check was a lot bigger than theirs. Glen responded by reducing my hours, first by pushing back my weekday starting time from 7:30, when the morning rush started, to 9:00, when business was slowing down. Then, since I was still making more than the mechanics who wanted to complain and smoke more than they wanted to work, they whined again to the boss. This time Glen told me to stop coming in on Saturdays, the busiest day of the week! At that point I said to him, "Look, Glen, I know what you are doing, so I'll just make this easy for you. You go ahead and run your store the way you want, and I'm gonna leave." He said to me, "If you leave, you'll never be eligible for a re-hire with Goodyear." I held my eyes on him and said, "Glen, someday I'm gonna come back and buy this store, and when I do, I'm gonna fire you." He laughed me off and went back to his paperwork. A few years later, I did buy that store, but Glen was already gone.

After leaving Goodyear toward the end of 1972, I decided to go into business for myself. Or, as they would say in my father's day, to "follow my own nose." My mother-in-law, Ellen, allowed me to borrow $20,000 on her house so I could lease the ARCO station at the corner of Clinton and West. My intention was never to sell a lot of gas like ARCO was expecting, but to build an auto-repair business using the hoists and other equipment available in the shop. I recruited some of the best workers from Glen Huntington's Goodyear store, including his service manager, his collector and repo man, and a recently hired mechanic who shared my work ethic. Glen was madder than a wet hen because he lost some of his best workers in a very short time, but I had my crew ready for opening day.

Before we opened, I went to a printer and ordered 15,000 fliers saying the ARCO station would be opening under new management, and that we would be offering oil changes, brake jobs, alignments, etc., each for such and such a price. Reneé and two local kids went door to door through the area with those fliers. After we opened, on January 3, 1973, the shop was busy from day one, and the business grew quickly.

Selling Goodyear tires out of the station was also part of my deal with ARCO. I was buying the tires from a wholesale distributor named Argain's Warehouse, and although no one ever taught me how to professionally sell a tire, I was good at it. About nine months after opening the ARCO station, with the tire and auto-repair business growing and good money coming in, I rented a 3,000 square foot garage about a half-mile away on Weber Avenue. I put together a small crew, moved some equipment into the garage, and named it *Shubin's Tire and Service Center*.

At that time, *ACE Service* had a contract with Firestone, and they had all the distribution from Grapevine to the Oregon border. I gave ACE a call and said I wanted to be a dealer with them. They sent a rep out to see me, and the interview went well. ACE agreed to give me some money for advertising and to put their identification on the building, and I became a dealer with them.

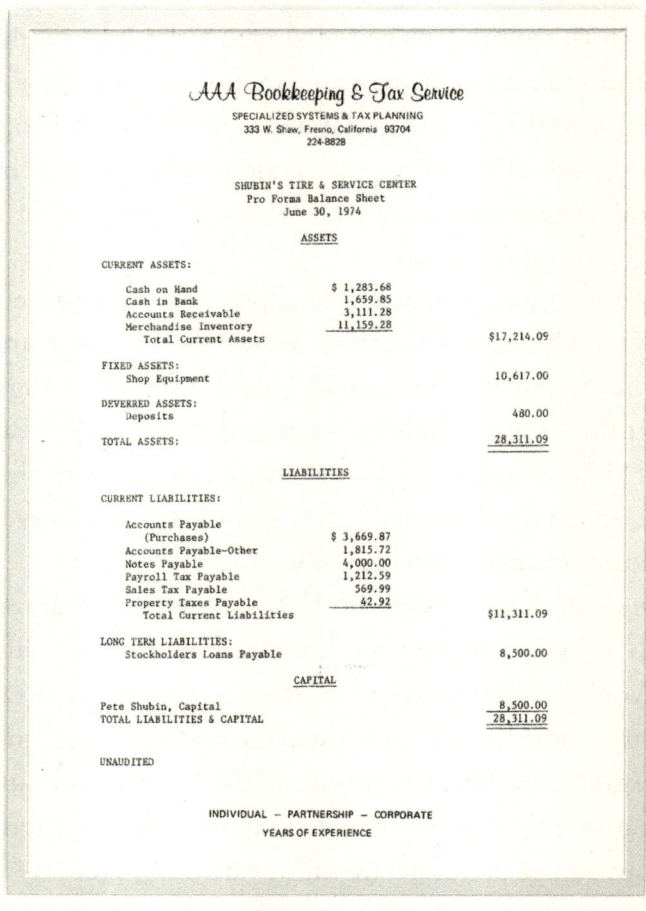

My financial status as of June 30, 1974

2502 N. Weber

At the Weber location I was able to focus on auto-repair and tire sales without the distraction of a gas island, so it seemed a good idea to get out of my two-year lease with ARCO and transfer all of my business to Weber. When I went to ARCO and asked to opt out of the lease, they turned me down. They said that until the lease expired in fifteen months, I had to continue receiving the amount of gas stipulated in the contract, and that I had to keep the station open each day until all of the gas was sold. Initially that was a disappointment, but little did we know that an oil embargo would hit in October, and gasoline would suddenly be in huge demand.

After the embargo hit, and cars were lined up and down the street waiting to buy gas, my lease with ARCO led to a unique opportunity. Don Klein, the owner of Klein's Truck Stop, approached me one day and said, "Hey, Pete, I know you want to get out of this station, and ARCO won't let you. How about if I just buy all of your gas at meter price, so I can sell it to the truckers [a little marked up, of course], and then you can close the station?" What this would mean for me is that I would sell all of my gasoline for the same price it would cost at the pumps, but I would not need to pay anyone to run the pumps! I agreed to the deal with Klein, and each time ARCO's tanker came to fill my storage tank, about an hour later Klein's truck would show up and suck it all out.

After this had been going on for a short while, the ARCO people would come by and say, "Why are you closed?" I would answer, "Because I haven't got any gas." When they asked what I did with all the gas, I would tell them, "I sold it." All was going well until one night an ARCO truck was filling my tank, and the Klein truck pulled up right behind it, a little early! That tipped off ARCO as to what I was doing, and they sent someone to secretly take pictures from across the street. After the ARCO people felt they had all their ducks lined up, they approached me and threatened to sue if I did not stop selling the gas to Klein. I said, "Hey, there's nothing in my contract that says *how* I have to sell my gas, as long as I'm selling it at meter price." I told them, "So you go ahead and sue, but you have to keep delivering the same amount of fuel until the lease is up!" When they realized I had turned the tables on them, they offered to let me out of the lease! Well, since I was making a nice profit selling all that gas without having to pay anyone to pump it, why should I want out of the lease? I moved the rest of my auto repair business down the street, and for about the last six months of the lease with ARCO, I used their station to wholesale my gasoline to Klein's Truck Stop, while focusing the rest of my time on building the auto repair business. I rarely opened the station, since I had no gas to sell, and all of my auto repair business was now on Weber.

When the ARCO lease expired in January of 1975, I moved my remaining equipment to *Shubin Tire and Service Center*. I was the salesman and head mechanic, doing more turning the wrench than administrative work. I had only a couple of employees, while Reneé did the accounting and I handled all the tire and auto repair sales. When we had downs, it was only because I had some bad habits with gambling and drinking. I would get invited to poker games with some of my car dealership customers, and instead of being responsible and saying no, I would be up half the night drinking and playing poker. We did not have a safe in the shop, so each day I left with all the cash in my pocket, and whatever I came back with the next day was my opening money. But even with my bad habits, the business grew rapidly, and my home life was warm and stable.

Backing up just a few months, another wonderful development took place in my life on October 22, 1974. My second dear son came into the world. We named him Craig Peter Shubin, and I was a very happy father. I remember buying a box of expensive cigars and passing them out to everyone at the shop. Craig was the cutest baby I had ever seen, and he started making a splash from the moment he was born. What I mean by that is, no sooner had he come out of the womb than he started peeing all over the doctor! To this day, I cannot keep from laughing each time I think about that. Like his brother Scott before him, and his brother Daniel after him, Craig was born with a dark complexion from the Cherokee blood in his mother. But whereas the others soon lost their dark complexion, Craig kept his, just like his grandfather on Reneé's side. I will have more to say about Craig and my other sons later in *My Life as I Remember It*, but let me say that I was really happy about having another son.

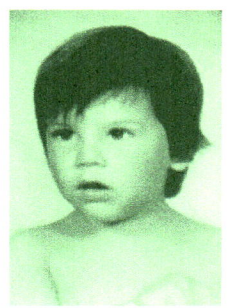

Scott, age 3   Craig, age 3

CHAPTER NINE
MIKE AND ROXIE

When Reneé graduated from high school and moved to Los Angeles, she initially lived with her father and his wife. This arrangement was not working out, and Reneé needed a more suitable living situation until we married. She worked at a stock brokerage firm in Beverly Hills, where she met a girl named Roxie Berger, who lived with her parents in Van Nuys. Roxie invited Reneé to move into her family's home, and for all of Reneé's time there, they treated her like their own daughter.

After we married and moved to Fresno, Roxie also moved there. She frequently babysat while Reneé and I went out for dinner or for a weekend. During those years, Roxie was always wanting us to meet her newest boyfriend, but it was the same old story with each one. Her boyfriends would eat my food, drink my booze, and then disappear so that I would never see them again. After the third or fourth time of this happening, I told Roxie I did not want to meet any more of her boyfriends. Well, one day in January of 1976, Roxie said she wanted us to meet her new boyfriend, Mike Foreman. I told her, "NO!" I said, "Roxie, all your boyfriends want to do is eat my food, drink my booze, and then I never see them again." She said that Mike was different, and she really wanted us to meet him. After she kept insisting, I broke down and told her,

"Okay, Roxie, I'll agree to meet him, but since I know I'll never see him again, I'm not even going to get dressed for the occasion." I told her that she and Mike could come over to our place for a barbeque, but that when Mike arrived, I would only be wearing my underwear. At first, she did not know if I was kidding or not, but of course I was. I also invited Roxie's cousin, Richard Berger, and his wife Jackie.

When the night came and they all arrived, Roxie's boyfriend was already half-drunk. At the first sight of him I thought he looked just like Tiny Tim, a long-haired singer from the 1960s. Mike told me he liked to drink Greyhounds (vodka and grapefruit), so I made him one, and then another, and then another. Hours later, after we had eaten and Mike was on his fourth or fifth Greyhound, he drunkenly slurred something like, "I don't think you like me." I told him, "I don't like any of Roxie's boyfriends. You eat my food and drink my booze, and after tonight I'll probably never see you again." Mike insisted that he was different and that he really loved Roxie. I said, "Do you love her enough to marry her?" He said, "I would marry her tonight if she would agree to it." After he said that, I motioned for Roxie to come and sit with us, and she did. When she was seated, I told her that Mike loved her and would marry her that very night if she agreed.

Mike and Roxie got up and went into another room to talk. After a short while, they came out and told me they had agreed to do it. By now it was nearly two o'clock in the morning, so maybe both of them were thinking they could say anything and then expect that nothing would actually happen. But next thing they knew, I was looking through the Yellow Pages to see where I could charter an airplane and have us all flown to Lake Tahoe for a Nevada-style wedding.

I called Skip's Charter Service and was told the only planes available were for six passengers, and that the pilot counted as one. This meant I would need to charter two planes to get all six of us there. I did it. At about four in the morning, Reneé and I got on one plane, the rest of our group got on the other, and off we flew to Tahoe.

The plane landed at about six in the morning, just as the day was dawning and the beauty of the area was coming alive right in front of us. I remember looking around at the tall trees and feeling in my lungs the cool, fresh breeze blowing across the snow. Since we knew that the courthouse in nearby Carson City would not open until ten, we went to a casino for some gambling. Mike quickly lost all his money, so he came to me saying he was broke and that he could not pay the fee for the marriage. It just so happened that I had won about the same amount he had lost, so I told him not to worry, that I had him covered. I could see he was getting nervous about all of this, and I did not want him backing out now. So, I got him a couple more Greyhounds, and after that, he was ready for Carson City.

We rented a car and drove to the courthouse, where Mike and Roxie got married. They stayed together until Mike died about twenty years later. Mike was a unique kind of guy, and you either liked him or you did not. He was rude and obnoxious most of the time, and you never saw him without his best friend, SIX PACK. But I personally liked the guy. He has been gone about twenty-five years now, and I still miss him.

CHAPTER TEN
THE MADERA STORE

A huge opening in my career came on June 9, 1976, three days before the birth of my third dear son, Daniel Peter Shubin. While Reneé and I eagerly awaited Daniel's birth, I happened to run into an old friend from high school named Richard Hobart. Richard told me about a Goodyear store in Madera where the manager, Ben Giuliano, was about to go under and wanted out of the business altogether. The more we talked about it, the better it sounded that I should buy that store. I wanted to be home with Reneé, but this was a huge opportunity for our future with a growing family, so I made the sacrifice and told Richard I was interested.

Richard called Ben, and we all agreed to meet that same night. After checking on Reneé, I drove to the address in Madera and met Ben, who turned out to be a news reporter by history. Goodyear put him into business only because he met their financial requirements, not because he had the experience or the ability to run a tire and auto repair store. Ben told me he had put $35,000 into the corporation and now, less than a year later, it was worth only $11,000. He said he owed Goodyear and others a total of about $100,000. He was clearly in over his head, and he said that if he could find somebody to buy him out for the net worth ($11K), he would sell it and go back to his old job as a news reporter in San Jose.

The next morning, I met with Ben and his attorney at the store. We did an inventory, and we did a total reconciliation of his accounts receivable/payable and his bank account. All I needed was $11,000 to buy the store. I did not have that, but Ben had $20,000 in the store's bank account, so I told him, "Ben, I'll buy your store. Let's sign." After he had signed his corporation over to me and handed me his company checkbook and credit cards, right in front of him I wrote myself an $11,000 bonus check and gave it to him as payment for the business. At first, Ben just stood there shaking his head. He turned to his lawyer and complained that something did not seem right about this, because I had just used *his* money to buy out *his* business! The attorney assured him that everything was legal, and on June 10th I took possession of the store. Two days later, my dear son Daniel was born. I now had three beautiful sons, and my career was rapidly taking off just at the time I would need the business success to provide for a growing family.

The Madera store had much more potential than the Weber store, and by the end of June I was doing more business in Madera than Ben had done in an entire year. I promoted an assistant, Richard Berger (Roxie's cousin, who had accompanied us to the wedding), to run the Weber store, while I concentrated on growing our business in Madera.

Everything was going well with the new location, until one day the Goodyear representative, Jack Rutherford, came by for a visit. I knew Jack from when I worked for Goodyear at the Fulton Mall, and after we greeted each other he said, "So, you're working for Ben?" I said, "No, I bought Ben out." Jack pulled back his head like he had just smelled something sour, and he said, "You can't do that!" He started lecturing me on how this is a Goodyear franchise tire center and that I need to first be approved as a franchisee, have my credit checked to make sure I'm creditworthy, and that I need to put thirty-five thousand dollars of unencumbered money into an account that Goodyear can verify. Jack assured me that all of this is "strict policy."

After he had finished his pompous speech, I said, "Well, Jack, what do you want me to do? Ben is not here. He's gone, and he's not coming back." I held my eye on his and explained that "I bought an existing corporation that Ben had already capitalized with thirty-five thousand dollars, but now it's not worth that much, so I bought it for the net worth and all we did is change officers in the corporation." I pointed out how "it's still the same corporation that Goodyear has already approved, and now I own it and I'm running it, and I know what I'm doing whereas Ben did not have a clue." I sort of clinched it by mentioning that "this business owes Goodyear a lot of money, but Ben would have been bankrupt in thirty days, and Goodyear would have gotten nothing." Jack started moving his lips around like he wanted to say something, but he did not know what to say, so he left. A few days later, he came back, with the district manager and a business counselor, and they tried to run the same story. When that did not work, they went back to their superiors, and next thing I knew some higher ups from Akron came and told me the same story all over again. Finally I said, "Look, here's the deal—I'm the new president of this corporation, and I know it owes you guys money, so let's set up a payment schedule and I'll pay you all that you're owed." I told them, "If you don't want that, well, the attorney who handled this transaction is right across the street. We can go over and see him, and we will just file for bankruptcy, and Goodyear will be out a hundred thousand bucks. Then I'll lock up the store and you won't be able to even get into it until you get me evicted maybe a year from now." I paused for a moment while they stared at me with stone-like faces, and then I said, "So let's work together on this."

One of the guys from Akron was a senior business manager, and he was not liking how this was going, but what could he say? He rubbed his chin and looked around for a minute, acting like he had different options to consider, when he knew he really did not. Finally, he said to me with a stiff face, "Okay Pete, but look, for us to sign off on this, you have to have something worth thirty-five thousand dollars unencumbered. Do you have anything?" I pointed to my toolbox and said, "Right there." Of course, the toolbox and the tools were not worth close to that amount, but the Akron person said to me, "Is it worth thirty-five thousand?" I nodded and said, "It's worth that much to me!" Right then and there they wrote a journal ticket that made my tools an asset of the corporation, valuing them at $35,000, and on that day Goodyear and I loved each other.

CHAPTER ELEVEN
EXPANDING

My career was expanding, and shortly after taking over the Madera store, I brought in a partner named Timothy Bagdonoff. Tim and I came from the same village in Iran and had sailed to America on the same ship. We shared a deep family history going back to the days in Russia when my father and Tim's grandfather labored together in a Stalinist prison camp, teaming up to provide decent burials for the prisoners who died under the harsh conditions. As Father tells it in his memoirs: *When somebody would die in the prison, we [Tim's grandfather and great uncle, along with my father] would bury them. No one wanted to do that because they considered it dangerous and dirty. So, we went and buried them, the three of us…He [Tim's grandfather] would tell me, 'Misha [Mikey], let's go bury these people, give them a decent burial, and for this we will get our reward some time.' (p. 21) …We went and buried and buried, and it became our job in the prison every day…although we were innocent and did nothing [wrong].* (p. 22)

Tim had no experience in the tire business, but he was a trusted friend and an honest person. He had experience in computer operations, which led me to think he would be helpful with the new move to computers in the business world, since I did not know the first thing about them.

As I mentioned in the previous chapter, I promoted Richard Berger to store manager at Weber, while I focused on Madera. Over the next few months, the numbers in Madera were very good, and I spent time training Tim, hoping to teach him what was needed so he could take over that store. Meanwhile, the numbers at the Weber location were falling, so when I thought Tim was ready, I turned the Madera store over to him, while I went to Fresno to find out why the numbers were falling.

While I was busy getting things back up to par in Fresno, the numbers started dropping in Madera. For a while, we had this teeter-totter between the two stores. When I focused on Fresno, the numbers in Madera fell, and when I shifted back to Madera, the numbers in Fresno fell. Finally, I decided it might be better to just sell the Weber store, figuring that someone working for himself would do much better than the manager I had.

About that time an old friend named John Gregorioff expressed interest in buying the Weber store. John was a salesman who did not know much about the automotive business, but his plan was to partner with his friend, Max Bebioff, a mechanic who worked for a car dealership. That sounded to me like a good plan, one man to handle sales and the other to work the shop. When John offered to pay what I wanted for the store, I sold it. Weber did about one-third the business of the Madera store, so I was glad to get it off my hands and concentrate on the better location.

In December of 1977, Tim and I bought a piece of property at 925 Clovis Ave. The Madera store was doing extremely well, with about ten times the business that Ben had been doing, so we felt well positioned and confident to approach Goodyear about building a store in Clovis. Goodyear agreed that if we built the store, they would franchise it and identify it without us needing to deposit an additional $35,000.

In June of 1978, we got approval from the city to start construction. I got busy, pouring a lot of finances, time and energy into the project. About sixty days before completion, I went to a district meeting in Sacramento where the Goodyear district manager, Ed Sprecht, told me very coldly that someone at Goodyear had made a mistake in approving me for a franchise at the Clovis location. He said an employee named Bob Hooper had already been approved for a location less than three miles from mine, so they had to turn down my application!

I said to Ed, "So, what am I going to do with my store, since it's almost ready to open and Bob Hooper hasn't even started construction?" He gave a little shrug and said, "All I can say is that we're sorry." I told him, "Well, it's actually okay with me if Goodyear doesn't identify me. I've got Firestone knocking at my door and they're chomping at the bit to get a dealer into the Clovis market."

Ed was not expecting that, and neither were his superiors at Goodyear. The last thing they wanted was a Goodyear franchisee with a tire center in Madera, also having a Firestone franchise in Clovis. Ed dropped his cold expression, and I could see he was trying to disguise how stupid he felt. Then he said, "Let me look into this." He left and came back a couple weeks later, telling me that Akron would make an exception to its own policy and approve me for the Clovis location. Two months later, on May 3, 1979, we opened for business.

The Clovis Store

While the Clovis store was under construction, Reneé and I decided we did not want our boys growing up in the city. After some looking around, we put a deposit on a home to be built on 2.5 acres in Wathen Estates, about four miles from the Clovis shop. Soon after this, the interest rates skyrocketed to a prime rate of 21%, and we were about to back out of the deal because we could not get a decent loan. One day Spaulding Wathen, the owner of the development, came to see us and said he had no doubt that interest rates would soon be coming down. He offered to finance our home at 10% interest, if we would commit to moving in when the house was done. That sounded good to us, so we sold our Fresno house and were able to move into the new home on November 1st, 1979.

Later in the next year, Goodyear had its blimp at the Fresno Fair. One day I was out there talking with the pilots, and they told me they needed to get the blimp up in the air to cool the helium. When they asked if I wanted to ride along with them, I said, "Yeah!"

Next thing I knew, I was flying over Fresno in the Goodyear blimp. After we had been up there a while, one of the pilots asked if there was anywhere in particular I wanted to go. I told him, "Yeah, let's go out by my house." Then he asked if I wanted to fly the blimp! I told him, "Yeah I want to fly the blimp!" Of course, the pilots were right there, paying very close attention to every move I made, but with their assistance, I lowered the blimp as far as they would let me over my home. The neighbors came running out of their houses to look, the dogs in the neighborhood all started barking, and the horses in the corrals took off running. That was a lot of fun, and boy, did I do some bragging. In 1950 I had left my Iranian village in a horse-drawn wagon, and thirty years later I was flying the Goodyear blimp over my custom-made home in California!

My kids grew up in that beautiful Clovis house, and I have a lot of good memories from there. Instead of being raised in a crowded city neighborhood, they were able to have mountain bikes and romp around in wide open spaces. After a while, we decided to build a large swimming pool. Timothy Bagdonoff recommended a guy by the name of Curt Stone, who had built the pool at Tim's home in Madera. I went and talked to Curt, and after he gave me a price estimate that was unbelievably low, I agreed to hire him to build the pool.

Work on the pool started out good, and we were all excited. Curt dug a hole shaped like the rim of a cowboy hat, 44 feet long and 44 feet wide. He put in the rebarb and finished the gunnite, but after that he stopped showing up regularly. When he did come to work, he kept asking for draws against the balance. I started smelling a rat, so one day I told him I would not give any more money until he did the plastering and started putting on the finishing touches. Well, after that I never saw Curt again. I think he realized he had badly underestimated the cost of building a pool that size, and that he was going to lose his butt on the deal. Curt fled the coop on me!

What happened next is that while I was busy with my stores, Reneé rolled up her sleeves and finished building the pool! She hired one of Curt's ex-workers to help her (I think he felt real bad about what Curt had done), and with the two of them going at it full-time, by Memorial Day of 1981 we were swimming in our own pool. Reneé and the boys were in it almost every day, and we started noticing that Scott and Craig had exceptional swimming skills. The boys often invited their friends for a swim, and sometimes I would come home and see about twenty kids splashing around in the pool.

All of this was during a time when I had to prove myself in business to support a family, and consequently my work took a lot of my focus. When I was a kid, I could not play Little League or be on a high school sports team, but I made sure my boys were able to do things like this, and even though I could not be there for many of their events, Reneé always attended and rooted the boys on.

We were like the Leave It to Beaver family, with Dad working and Mom at home, involved in all the kids' activities. We also took a lot of vacations, traveling to places like Hawaii and the Caribbean. One special memory I have is our winter-time tradition of standing reservations at Lake Tahoe between Christmas and New Year's. We would hit different ski resorts for six days straight, and boy did we have a blast. Life was good, business was strong, and time rolled forward.

My three sons!

Craig with his grandfather

CHAPTER TWELVE
MOTHER

At work and with home life, things were going very well. I was in my early thirties, with a wonderful wife and three beautiful sons, a nice house in the country and a business that paid for it all. But a time was coming which almost everyone has to face, sooner or later.

Mother had been sick and was not getting better. For a while we did not know why she was feeling ill, but then she turned jaundice and her doctor sent her to a specialist. At the hospital they opened her up, and when they saw how badly the pancreas was swollen, they just closed her up and told my dad she had pancreatic cancer and there was nothing they could do. This was hard for all of us, but mostly of course for Father, who needed to prepare for life without his loyal companion of fifty years.

In loving desperation, Father took Mother to Mexico where they tried Laetrile for three months. Mother was back and forth each month, even though she was suffering very badly, and after all of that, the Laetrile did not help. Linda and Vera took most of the care of her, while us boys stayed close to Father.

Even though Mother was so sick, she wanted to see my Clovis store, which she knew I had built from the ground up. One day Father brought her, and I gave her a tour of the store. She told me how proud she was, and she blessed me for all that I had accomplished.

My dear mother passed on November 16, 1979. It was only two weeks after we had moved into our new home, and she never got to see it. Toward the end of that month, the family all came to my house for Thanksgiving, but it was different without Mother there.

After her passing, Father was very lonely out on the farm. Sometimes he would show up at my door unannounced, just wanting to have some company. I try to imagine how it was for him, after a half-century together and all they had been through. Father's Memoirs express how deeply he missed Mother, as he himself tells it:

I am home alone this time. As I told you in the beginning about a song, "My life comes to me like a flower blooms, but now it has wilted and is sorrowful (p104)." Living life alone is hard, you leave alone, you come back alone, and nobody asks you, "Where are you going?" or "When will you return?" (p. 104)...

For me this was so very hard. Why hard? Because we lived 50 years in peace, love, friendship, companionship, agreement, always we were one. We always came to one decision, it was ours ...

It was so extremely hard for us, again, no words to explain the waiting for the time to pass and for Mother to go away from us and we have to bury her. For 5/6 months, exactly like the doctor said, you guys heard him. The day did come. Mother passed away on 11/16/1979... Quite often this song comes to mind, "Oh, how I cry out and bitterly sob." (p. 93)

Father and Mother (c. 1930)

Vera behind Mom and Dad, with Bill, Jim and Alex in front (c. 1945)

Shubin family, New York (c. 1951)

Mother and Aunt Raya

Mother and Dad were like a couple of doves, sitting on a wire and mating for life. When they had married, back in Russia in 1930, they did not first court and then wed after "falling in love." As Father explains in his Memoirs:

When I turned 21, my grandfather came over and they were sitting, he and my father, having lunch and talking, and then the conversation turned to me. Grandfather said to me, sitting next to my father, "You need to find a bride." Grandfather left and father then said to me again, "You need to find a bride."

So in those days, when your father says, "find a bride," you don't talk back or talk about it, you just do it... So I found a bride. The bride I found was your mother. I picked her. I did it. Not like you guys do it here, courting for 1-2 years. They told me to "pick one" so I did...and in one week it was a done deal. We were married...on March 14, 1930.

My parents were old fashioned, and Mother was used to how things were in the old days, when the man got the horses and wagon ready and the woman rode along beside him. Together, they left behind an amazing story.

I remember one day when Mom said to my wife, "Reneé, can you take me to the doctor and interpret for me?" That was cute, because Reneé could barely speak Russian, and Mother could barely speak English, so how could Reneé interpret? When Mother realized what she was asking, they both got a good laugh from it, but they went to the doctor together and somehow made it work.

My mother was a beautiful woman, and I have wonderful memories of her from as far back as I can remember. When we were little, she used her own hands to lovingly make the clothes we wore. I do not know how she made them fit so well, but she did. She was also an excellent cook and could feed a group of people on a moment's notice. Because of all the canning she did during the summer, our freezer was full of good things to eat. Dad could bring home half the congregation from church, and Mother would have a way of preparing something for everybody. She also used milk from our cow to make our own butter, sour cream, yogurt and buttermilk. We rarely had store-bought food, except occasionally some pasta or bread, but everything else she made and cooked herself. I do not know how she found time for it all. She was just an incredible woman.

Mother and Father, 1970's

CHAPTER THIRTEEN
AN INDEPENDENT TIRE DEALER

Meanwhile, things went on with life and work. I left Tim at the Madera store while I concentrated on Clovis, and the new venture started growing from day one. We had spent nearly $400,000 getting that store ready, and within a few months it started paying for itself. In the years to come, our Clovis location would consistently rank either first or second (in service, tire sales and tire units) out of approximately fifty Goodyear locations in the Sacramento district.

Around the beginning of 1980, the new Goodyear regional manager, Max Schrimsher, came out to see me. We agreed to meet for dinner at Reuben's Restaurant. Max came with three of his guys (the district manager, the business counselor, and the area salesman), and I came with Tim. Max had a reputation for being brutal with his employees, and right there at the table he started in on me about selling products that were not from Goodyear. He began talking to me like I was an employee in violation of company rules, when in fact I was an independent dealer who happened to do a lot of business with Goodyear.

After about a minute of letting Max blow steam, I reached into my pocket and pulled out the keys to the Madera store. I stood and said, "Max, here's the keys to the store," and I threw them on the table in front of him. As I turned to walk away, I told him, "If you think you can do a better job running the store, then you do it." I went out and sat at the bar, and a few minutes later Max came and apologized. He told me he had to use that kind of language in front of his employees, and I told him I am not his employee, that I work for myself. Then he tried saying it was because of his German temperament and upbringing, or something like that, and how it makes him want to always control the conversation in front of his people. I looked at him and said, "Well, this is my *Russian* temperament." I started to tell him, "We froze you guys out once at Leningrad," and that brought a laugh from both of us.

After my joke had lightened things up between us, I got serious and said, "Max, I've taken that store from bankruptcy to the point that I'm buying millions of dollars of product from you guys. What is the big deal if I sell something other than a Goodyear tire because a customer wants it? I'm not going to send a customer down to a competitor because the customer wants that particular tire. That is what it takes to run a business. If you want me to run the store, I'll run it for you. If you don't, you've got the keys." He gave a rough smile, then handed me back the keys and said, "You're doing a good job." We shook hands and went back to the table.

At this time, my career really started to take off. I went from running one store in Madera to opening five locations in 18 months. I was more focused on service than on selling tires, but without realizing it I was on my way to becoming the largest independent tire distributor from the Grapevine to Sacramento.

I had sold the Weber store to John Gregorioff and his partner, Max Bebioff, in 1978, but after a couple of years, Max moved on.

John started having a rough time running the store, and he was struggling to pay me for the purchase. I still owned the lot next to the store, so one day in 1980 I approached John and said, "I know you're having a hard time paying me. Instead of me foreclosing on you, why don't we just agree that Tim and I will take over your corporation and build a brand new store on the vacant lot, and we'll give you a minority partnership into that location." John agreed, so we took over that corporation. I had some plans drawn up for a store next door, and when it was built, we let John run it as a small minority owner under our jurisdiction.

2530 N Weber

One day in November of 1981, not long after opening the new Weber store, I was driving down Blackstone and I noticed the tire store in the Mervyn's shopping center was closing. The store was operated by a company called Mchatton Tire, which did mostly wholesale tire business. I immediately called Mervyn's and was told the store's current dealer was going out of business, and the location was available. The next day I drove to San Leandro to meet with the real estate department, and they told me I could have that location if I would take over the existing lease, which had about ten years left on it.

The Mervyn's Store

I took the deal on that store and was very happy with it, but Goodyear was not happy because they had a company-owned store only a half-mile down the street (on Blackstone and Dakota). When Goodyear tried putting pressure on me about this, instead of giving up my opportunity at Mervyn's, I answered that I had already signed the lease and it was a done deal on my part. In business, I have found that if I really believe in something, I do not have to let anything intimidate me. Goodyear was accustomed to seeing their franchisees fold under pressure from on top, but I told them

I was going to invest in cleaning up and remodeling the location, and that I was going to open it up as a tire store. I said, "If you want me to sell Goodyear tires there, then you need to make an exception to your location policy and identify it." After a lot of back and forth between me and the district office, they persuaded Akron to make another exception and identify the store with a *Goodyear Tire* sign. It was back to love between me and Goodyear.

Not long after I opened the store at Mervyn's, Goodyear started having a hard time at their store down the block (on Blackstone and Dakota). In September of 1982, they called and wanted to know if I was interested in buying it. I told them I would, but only if they left all their equipment inside and their identification on the outside. They agreed, and I bought the location for a very reasonable price. Even though I now had two stores only a block from each other, I had a good manager in each one, and both locations started doing very well. Our business now had a total of five stores.

3877 N. Blackstone

Around this time, I approached Goodyear about getting off their franchise program and becoming what is called a G110 dealer. My business volume had reached such a level that I was paying $350,000 a year in royalty fees. As a G110 dealer, I would still be involved with Goodyear, but I would not have to pay them anything. There were changes that would come with being a G110 dealer (such as no longer having a business counselor assigned to me), but it would save a lot of money.

Goodyear fought me on the G110 request, until one day I went to a district meeting where they announced that anyone who wanted out of their franchising program could do so. (I later found out that Goodyear had never been licensed to sell franchises in California at all!) After that meeting, I was the first to drop out of the program and become an independent dealer.

About a year later I also asked Goodyear to let me off their national advertising program, since the national rates which my stores had to pay were twice what I would need to pay for local advertising. It did not take a high dollar business counselor to figure that one out. Goodyear would not budge, and they fought me on this for a long time. One day Max Schrimsher, who had now become the Goodyear vice-president, made a trip to visit me. I laid out Goodyear's national advertising program rates with the Fresno Bee, and then I laid out the local rates in the same newspaper. Goodyear was paying about $92 an inch, and they would co-opt fifty percent of it, meaning that I was still liable for $46 an inch. I told Max that I could buy the same ad space locally for $38 an inch and Goodyear would still have to co-opt it, meaning it would cost me only $17 an inch. Max agreed, and he said that Goodyear would go ahead and consider my operations to be regional rather than local, and that they would take me off their advertising program. That was another step forward for my business.

CHAPTER FOURTEEN
LEGAL MESS

One day in 1982 I was approached by a man who identified himself as a reporter from ABC's popular news show, Nightline. His name, as well as I can remember, was Peter Laszewski, and he started his pitch by describing a book entitled *Mr. Badwrench*, supposedly about dishonesty and the exploitation of consumers in the auto-repair business. Laszewski said he had researched the growth of my company and was impressed, and that he believed my stores were a reversal of the negative profile of the industry presented in the book. He asked if he could interview me as an example of honesty and integrity in the auto repair business, and I agreed.

I have always taken my business ethics seriously and have always felt concern for the general public to know there are many honest and reliable people in the auto repair industry. When the day came for the interview, I felt upbeat and eager to give a truthful presentation of how an auto service business can be successful without resorting to unethical tactics.

The interview started well, but then Laszewski broadsided me with an abrupt change of tone. He pushed out his chin and tilted his head slightly to the right, then he said something like, "Our people have been filming your store from the Mervyn's shopping center across the street." He paused for a moment, like he wanted his words to sink in, but I was baffled as to why he would want to film my store. When I did not say anything or show any expression of concern, he asked me a question, but in a way that a lawyer might speak to a person on a witness stand. He said, "Why do you sell shock absorbers to customers who do not need them?" I felt like he had just spit in my face, so I leaned forward and said, "What are you talking about? We don't do that!" He lifted his chin even higher, and with a smirk on his skinny mouth, he started telling me he has on camera multiple cases where his people smeared oil on shock absorbers, so that the absorbers needed nothing more than to be cleaned, but instead, my store had sold the customers new ones. "Why does your business do that?", he said.

I told him, "My business does not deliberately do that. When a car comes in with leaky shocks, we do not take them off to test them. If the shocks are saturated with oil, we assume they are leaking."

Laszewski acted like he had not even listened to my words. Immediately he said, "We have, on film, cases of a customer coming to your store with one bad tire, and instead of selling him a new tire, your store sells him a pair!" He was slightly raising his voice, again like a lawyer building his case in a courtroom, and with the cameras rolling. Before I could answer, he threw in my face another allegation, saying his people had sent in a car with a wire disconnected in a not-so-noticeable place in the alternator, and instead of my store finding and reconnecting the hidden wire, we sold the customer a new alternator.

The Nightline people had been baiting us by sending in cars that had been cleverly altered to give the appearance of damage. On the surface, this looked bad for me, but there is an old saying, "A person's story sounds good, until you hear the other person's side." There were legitimate answers to each point Laszewski was bringing, but I was not prepared for this. I did my best to explain that radial tires need to be replaced in pairs, to eliminate radial tire pull. Then I explained that when a car comes in with a charging problem, the first thing we do is test the alternator, rather than search for hidden wires that somebody might have disconnected upstream.

The book that was used as a ruse.

If I had been given a fair chance, I could have embarrassed Nightline with evidence refuting every charge they were making. But Laszewski and his people had put too much into this, and they were not interested in "fair chances." This is their business, and they are out to win, so it was clear to me that they were working on wrong assumptions but had no interest in answers that did not line up with what they already believed. I had worked hard to build my business, and I required from my employees not only quality work, but also a high ethical commitment. Standing there in front of Laszewski, with the cameras pointed directly at me, I felt I had been set up and misrepresented. I slightly raised my voice and said something like, "It seems to me that *you* are the one who is a crook and doing fraudulent stuff." I pointed out how he had conned me into this interview relating to a book called Mr. Badwrench, telling me he saw me as the reverse side of what the book was profiling, and now I learn that his story was all lies and manipulation. I ended the interview by walking out while they were still filming.

After the interview, I wondered why Nightline had singled me out like this. I knew that my salesmen and mechanics were honest in representing our business, so we got busy looking into the matter, to learn what we could about why they had placed us in their crosshairs.

In a fairly short time, we learned that Nightline was working in conjunction with the Bureau of Automotive Repair, and that an ex-employee whom we had fired for stealing, had fabricated charges against us. It would take a while for my business to be cleared, and for me to learn the full story of why all of this was happening. But on the day of that interview, I could only do my best by giving honest answers to what looked at first sight like serious misbehavior at my store. This incident was the beginning of a very rough period that would last for years and would teach me a lot about keeping up my guard in the business world. (Also, I later heard that Nightline ran the story on the East Coast and in the mid-West, but then a war broke out in the Middle East and ABC decided the war was more newsworthy than my story.)

Not long after the Nightline interview, the District Attorney's office served me with a summons containing 31 complaints from customers over a six-year period, from 1976-82. Because of the size of the document, I was asked to pick it up rather than having it mailed to me. I immediately called my attorney, Dennis Neudek, who escorted me to the D.A.'s office, along with his associate, Walter Johnson. Since by now we had been tipped off that the Bureau was behind this, and since we knew the Bureau loves to play up to the media, we expected the news people to be there. When we got to the building, Dennis and I took the stairs while Walter took the elevator to answer questions with the media.

Our stores had written more than a quarter-million invoices during that six-year period, and out of the 31 complaints (which we had known nothing about), most were no more than paperwork violations, like doing work for a customer without a signature, or failing to record a license plate number. After all the nonsense issues had been weeded out, we were left with thirteen real complaints.

On November 7, 1984, we settled with the D.A.'s office for a $25,000 fine and a three-year probation. The Bureau was furious, claiming they had spent over $100,000 on the investigation, but there was nothing more they could do at the county level. I suspected we had not heard the last of it.

CHAPTER FIFTEEN
GOODGUYS

While all of that had been going on with the Bureau and the District Attorney's Office, we pushed on with growing our business. In November of 1983, Goodyear asked if I was interested in taking over their store at the Fulton Mall. This is where I had started with them after moving back to Fresno in 1972, working for Glen Huntington, the manager whom I promised to fire when I came back and bought that store. Unfortunately, Glen had already moved on.

Fulton was a big location with 10,000 square feet, ten bays, and a big warehouse that could hold over 5,000 tires. It never did well for us as a business, because the downtown area was drying up and nearly all the major stores in the mall had already moved out. I got it more for the big warehouse, but it was one store I should not have bought. We used it to stock tires that we did not have room for in other stores, and the showroom was big enough to partition off and move our accounting office into. We also used the location for a small wholesale business and a parts department, mostly delivering to our own stores.

Not long after opening for business at Fulton, I started buying tires from a Goodyear competitor (Dunlop Tire) at a very good price. One day the Goodyear representative, John Briceno, walked in through the back door and saw the Dunlop tires. He reported me to the district manager, Rich Gibbons, whom I had gotten along with very well. Gibbons wrote me an extremely nasty letter, certified from him, telling me in strong language how unhappy he was about the Dunlop tires in my warehouse. Gibbons reminded me of all the things Goodyear had done for me, and he said that when my leases run out, they will not be renewed (he never followed through on the threat). He did not mention what I had done for Goodyear, taking over a nearly bankrupt company that was on credit hold, and turning it into a business now buying three million dollars of product a year from them.

About that time, I made the decision to dump the Goodyear accounting system. When I had started taking over their troubled locations, I quickly learned they did not have a consolidated accounting system or a balance sheet that balanced all of the stores as one company. By now, my own company had grown to a half-dozen stores with nearly a hundred employees, and my accountant, Ted Starkel, had to use a system not designed for multiple tire operations. Sometimes we took double and triple extensions on filing tax returns, because nothing ever balanced with the antiquated system we were using.

With no way to track multiple locations, it was hard to really know if we were making a profit as a whole. We could look at one store and say, 'Yeah, we made a profit there,' but we did not have a consolidated number that balanced accounts among all the stores. Finally, we decided to shop around for a new computer system. Timothy Bagdonoff had been a computer operator at an assembly plant for Ford Motor Company, but that was before personal computers, so he really did not know much about what we needed.

One day I went to the SEMA Show in Las Vegas (an automotive after-market show), knowing they always have people from computer companies at those events. While I was there, I got to talking and having drinks with a salesman named Doug Winters from Computers Northwest. He showed me his system, and as we kept drinking, he kept working on me. After the third or fourth drink, we shook hands and agreed that he would deliver a quarter-million-dollar computer system to my office in Fresno.

A short time later, the system arrived, but Doug's corporate then realized he had sold it without a deposit! When he called and told me his people wanted to get paid for their system, I said, "Look, Doug, you delivered the system, but how the heck does this thing work?" I told him they had just dropped this on my lap, and I needed someone to come out and hook it up. He quickly sent some people out, and after they got the whole thing up and running, Doug flew to Fresno where I met him at the airport and handed him the check for a quarter-million-dollars. He held the check in his hand and looked at it, nodded his head and stared at it, and then finally he said something like, "How do I know this is good?" I told him, "Just hang on to it for a couple days until I can get a loan!" He looked at me like he was having a bad dream, but in the end it all worked out, and we now had a computer system that would change how we do business.

The mainframe had all the ingredients of what I needed, but there was no one to teach me how to implement them. Just like no one ever trained me in how to run a business or sell a tire, I also had no training in accounting or in building programs on computers. I had to educate myself as to what I wanted the system to show me, so I started with the basics, like teaching myself how to read a balance sheet and how to set up a computer program for a balance sheet. That was about a three-year process, working my way through it line by line, day by day. It did not come easy, but I stayed with it until I got it.

Under the old system, when a set of tires was sold, we had to key in each piece of revenue that is attached to selling a set of tires, like wheel balancing, alignment, valve stems and road hazard warranty. But now it all came up automatically, so the clerk did not have to sit there and punch in, and punch in, and punch in product codes to get them on the invoice. That is what Goodyear did with its system. They would take the tires first, then the valve stems, then the wheel balancing, and so on. Everything had to be done individually.

With our new system, for example, having a program for a balance sheet, each month I could say, "I've got a net worth of a million dollars," and the balance sheet would show me where it came from. It would show all the assets against the liabilities, balanced to the penny. (The balance sheet is a consolidation of assets against liabilities, and the two figures need to balance.)

I also built a program that enabled me to see where all my company's sales were coming from. After that, I built a program that provided a sales analysis report for each individual store, along with a consolidated report for all of them. I never had that before. Then I did the same with accounts receivable. Instead of needing to look at multiple sets of accounts receivable, the program had one account for each customer no matter how many stores he purchased products at. For example, a customer with an account at our Fulton Mall store could go to any one of our locations and bill his purchase to that account. When I looked at accounts receivable, it would show me which stores the customer made his purchases at.

The system also did not have a profit/loss statement, and most of my accounting-system education came from building one and designing it for what I wanted it to show me. A profit/loss statement is like a road map to get me where I want to go, without getting lost in the process. With no road map, a person can get lost awful easy and end up anywhere. But with a consolidated profit/loss statement, balance sheet, inventory, accounts payable and accounts receivable, I always knew where my company stood as a whole.

I also created a budgeting program which showed each store manager what the expectations were in tire sales, wheel balancing, road hazard warranty, parts sales, labor sales, etc. Without having some sort of guide in front of them every day, the managers would not know what the expectations were. Every month I paid bonuses for those who met or exceeded the expectations laid out in the budget.

Getting that new system up, and learning how to build the right programs within it, was a big step forward for our company, and also for me as a businessman.

Another major development from those years was creating my own trademark name. After dropping out of Goodyear's franchise program, I could still use the name *Goodyear*, but not in conjunction with *Tire Center* (their trademark name). I could name my stores *Pete's Goodyear* or *Fresno Goodyear* or any other kind of *Goodyear*, but I could not use their full trademark name. So, what did I do? Well, I was not going to give Goodyear the satisfaction of having their name on my buildings at all. I spoke with Dunlop, who had been selling me a lot of tires, and they agreed to come and change the identification on my stores from *Goodyear Tire Centers* to **Goodguys Tire Centers**. By changing only four letters (from *year* to *guys*), no other changes in spacing or design were needed, and that saved a lot of money in putting up new identification at each of the stores.

Then one day I asked my advertising agent if he knew somebody who did customized logos, and he referred me to a company that showed me three or four different options to choose from. I changed the logo to:

Goodguys logo

Today the *Goodguys* tire chain is more recognized than Goodyear in the Fresno area. On each store the logo is the same. We no longer use *Goodyear* on any of our signs.

CHAPTER SIXTEEN
THE MID-EIGHTIES

The Bureau of Automotive Repair pushed their case against us up to the State Attorney General's Office, which had the authority to take away my business license. The Bureau was trying to run me out of the automotive business altogether, and they used their status and resources to bring in the media. At one point, I hired a Private Investigator to send people into the Bureau's office with fake complaints, some against our company, and some against others. What the P.I. found was that when someone complained about a company other than ours, the lead investigator, Darrell Penner, would say something like, "Did you try to take it up with that company before coming here to make it a legal problem with the Bureau?" If the person said, "No," then Penner would say, "You should go back to the company and first try to resolve this matter with them." But when one of the plants said the complaint was against *Goodguys*, Penner would say, "Fill out this form, and sign under penalty of perjury that you are telling the truth, and we will handle the rest of it."

The Bureau did not know we were accumulating this evidence of wrongdoing in their Fresno office, and they were hammering us on television, in the newspapers, and on radio. At one point in the mid-1980s, the bad publicity was costing us about forty percent of our business. It was a rough period, and the entire mess was a huge distraction on my time and concentration.

Meanwhile, we kept pushing on with our business, and I was a rising star in the eyes of Goodyear because of the amount of products we purchased from them. In September of 1984, Max Schrimsher included me on a list of dealers whom Goodyear invited to the Indy 500 Speedway and to meet A.J. Foyt. We were supposedly the up-and-coming dealers in the eyes of the Goodyear organization. Reneé packed me to the hilt for that three-day occasion. Because I am not a fancy dresser, and she did not want me to embarrass her, she included a suit and tie, which I dutifully wore.

At Indianapolis, Goodyear put us up at the Indy 500 Hotel, which is right on the track. The next day we went out to the track and walked through the garages where the teams were busy working on their cars and testing them. That was an amazing experience, to be right down there where it all takes place. Also, we went on a tour of the Indianapolis Museum and saw some of the Indy cars that have won the race since the Speedway first opened in 1909.

The next day we spent time at the track with A.J. Foyt, who put on a little demonstration to show us how well the Goodyear tires worked. Then, Goodyear brought out the Indy pace car, a Pontiac Fiero beefed up to exceed 200 miles per hour. A.J. took each of us on a high-speed, four-lap ride around that most famous racetrack in the world. When it was my turn to get into the souped up pace car, the president of Goodyear had just gotten out. I had heard that A.J. was short-tempered, and I picked up on his sarcasm when he said to me, "I guess you want me to go sixty-five miles an hour too, huh?" What had happened is the Goodyear president did not want to go faster than the normal freeway speed limit, and that did not sit too well with A.J. Foyt on the Indy 500 Raceway! I said to him, "A.J., I'm here to have fun. Let's go balls to the walls." After I said that, he changed his temperament and became very friendly.

Me with AJ Foyt

With the PPG girls at Indy

On the track!

Well, I knew I was getting into a fast car, but I did not know we were going to do 214 miles an hour! At one point, as we were coming up on turn four, he said, "Look, I'm going to show you how good these tires work." I watched in amazement as he put one fingertip on each side of the steering wheel and said, "I'm going to hit this turn at one-hundred and eighty-six miles an hour with no hands on the wheel, and we're going to come out of the turn at two-hundred and fourteen." Then he did it. I about pooped my pants. My elbow was hanging out the window, and I swear it must have rubbed the wall. It was that close. When we came to a stop, he said, "How was that?" I said, "Great, but do you have some clean underwear!" A.J. got a good laugh from that, and then I told him, "Let's do it again!" He smiled and said, "Okay," and off we went for an extra lap.

Goodyear also brought in the Pacific Plate and Glass girls, about eight of them. Each of the girls had a different car, designed to do different things. One car that I remember, and which I rode in, was a Corvette that did not have any windows and was completely driven by a computer operated by a PPG girl inside the car. Later that night we had dinner with A.J. and the girls, and it was all a lot of fun, the whole three-day affair. When I got back home, I had a lot of stories to tell.

Meanwhile, our business continued to pick up, even while the mess with the Bureau was demanding a lot of my time and focus. One day in October of 1985, I called Goodyear about a store they had closed on Kings Canyon and Chestnut in Fresno. Goodyear had moved out and left all their equipment inside. I called and said that if I decided to open their store, could I have the equipment that was already there? After some back and forth, they agreed to sell me the equipment for a depreciated value, about $5,000.

I bought the store and reopened it under the *Goodguys* logo. We now had six stores operating under that name.

Life at home was stable and happy in those years. Scott was excelling on his high school water polo team, and we were wondering if he might end up with a scholarship. Craig had moved from Elementary School to Junior High, and we noticed he was outgrowing the slow, hand-eye coordination that had caused a lot of challenges for him at school. We also noticed he was developing a strong skill in talking with people. Man, this kid could sell snow to an Eskimo! What really gave him the opportunity to show this talent was after we got him a CB radio and he put a big antenna on the roof. Next thing we knew, he was talking to people in Australia and then all over the world!

Danny also excelled in water polo and swimming

Scott on a Tahoe slope

About that time, I began to be unhappy with my business partner, Tim. As I mentioned in an earlier chapter, he was a trusted friend and an honest person, and that never changed. But what did change is the closeness we had, and his value to me in the business. Part of the problem was that I had left the Molokan church at a young age, whereas Tim stayed in it. About a year after I married Reneé, Tim married Debbie, who was also a Molokan, and for a long time we still hung out together, even visiting at each other's homes when our kids were little. This started to change about the time Scott became a teenager, and when Tim moved from Madera and bought a new house in Fresno, he never invited us over. More importantly, as far as the partnership went, when we expanded into more and more stores in the mid-1980s, Tim was of less and less help to me. I complained about this to Reneé, and she advised that I talk with him about a buyout. But soon I would experience some major upheavals in my life, and it would be many years before I pursued the idea of buying out Tim.

CHAPTER SEVENTEEN
SADNESS AT HOME

One day in 1986 I was in the middle of a parking-lot sale at our Mervyn's store, waiting for Reneé to arrive and help with some things. She had told me she was first going to stop at Saint Agnes Hospital to visit her mother, Ellen, whom we expected to soon be released by the doctors after treatment for a certain illness. Well, suddenly I got a call from Reneé, and before she could say two words, she broke down sobbing. "What's wrong?", I said, with my chest slightly tightening because I knew this could not be good news. With the commotion all around me in the parking lot, I listened to Reneé explain that when she had walked up to her mom's bedside, she was not breathing. "She's dead," my wife said, with her voice breaking in the middle of the second word. That news hit hard. Someone so special in our life, just gone. It is something, how our day can be going along so normal, and then suddenly it all changes. Reneé told me that the nurses had not noticed any warning signs, but it turned out that all along she had a blood clot. The clot traveled into Ellen's lung and killed her before anyone could even notice she was in trouble.

My mother-in-law was a really nice person whom I had known for more than twenty years. She had divorced when Reneé was young and had never remarried. Her great ambition in life was to raise her girl, and the two of them were more like sisters than like mother and daughter. I met Ellen when she was almost fifty, and I do not recall her and I ever having an argument. Because she was single, we would take her to all of our family functions, and my family members also treated her with respect. As I mentioned in an earlier chapter, Ellen helped me launch my career by letting me borrow $20,000 on her house so I could lease the ARCO station in 1973.

Losing Reneé's mom was tough for us, but little did I know that for the next couple of years, I would be going from one funeral to another.

The next blow came in 1987. During the school year we had hosted a foreign-exchange student named Carlos Beccar, whose family invited us to their home in Bolivia after Carlos graduated. I could not get away at that time, but Reneé went, taking Craig with her. On the second or third day, my wife came down with dysentery, an infection in the intestines that normally lasts only a few days. When the doctors there could not stop the dysentery, Reneé called and told me she was coming home early.

I made an appointment with our family doctor, and when Reneé returned we went to his office for an exam and for some blood tests. After that, as the days passed and we waited for the results, Reneé was not getting any better. One day the doctor called and told us the blood tests had come back. We were glad to hear that, but then he told us he was referring Reneé to an oncologist. When we heard him say, "oncologist," it took a couple seconds to sink in. We were young, and Reneé at that time was only thirty-seven. She looked so healthy, so beautiful, so alive. How could she have cancer?

The call from the doctor was disturbing, and we decided not to tell the boys until we found out more. A few days later, we went to the oncologist for more tests, and then we waited. One day we got a call from the oncologist's office, asking us to come back. We went immediately, and when we got there, the specialist took us into a room. After we were seated, he began explaining to us that Reneé had a very rare form of cancer called *Plasma Cell Leukemia Multiple Myeloma*. After telling us a few things about this, he did his best to speak gently as he said to Reneé, "I am sorry to tell you that there is no known cure, and you have nine or ten months to live." Once those words came out of his mouth, my first thought was to be strong for my wife, but I felt like I had just fallen off a cliff.

The oncologist told us this kind of cancer was basically an old person's disease, and that it was basically a man's disease, and primarily an old black man's disease. Reneé did not fit any of those categories, and she had no history of cancer on either side of her family. To this day, it is a troubling mystery to me, and at times I have struggled with the idea that I was punished for not appreciating my wife the way I should have.

The oncologist advised us that he could order treatment and regulate it locally, or he could put Reneé on a study with the University of Arizona, which was the only place in the country that had studies on that particular cancer. Reneé's blood samples would be sent to Arizona and the doctors there would be in charge of her treatment. Either way, the oncologist made clear that there was no known cure. Reneé' made the decision to go with the University medical team, not because it held out any hope, but basically for how the studies might benefit others in the future.

Boy did that change our lives. We grasped for second opinions, and we prayed a lot for a miracle. At one point we drove to Stanford University, desperately hoping for a different diagnosis, but when we got there, the meeting was very short. The doctors from Fresno had sent the blood work, and Stanford had already done their own analysis, so there was not much else for them to do. A doctor took us into a private room and did his best to gently tell us that Reneé' in fact had Plasma Cell Leukemia Multiple Myeloma, and that there was very little hope.

During the drive home, we talked about the boys and how we would bring this to them. Later that day, we gathered them together and gave them the news. They all just stood there speechless. Nobody knew what to say, but we did our best to comfort and encourage them.

After that, each week we had Reneé's blood sent to Arizona, and she started chemotherapy. The months rolled by, and amazingly she did not lose any of her hair from the chemo. But the decline was visible. My wife was dying, and I could not do anything about it, except to make her as comfortable as possible. I had never felt so helpless in my life, and it greatly affected my focus at work.

In October of 1987, about three months after Reneé's diagnosis, my sister Vera's husband, John Volkoff, died. John was very close to my father and had always been a big part of my family's life. He had been raised in an orphanage in Russia and never knew his own father, but my dad was a father to him. Dad spoke of John in his Memoirs, referring to him as "our God-given son" and urging us to "don't ever forget" him:

But, we thank God, we had... your sister [Vera] and our God-given son, Ivan Vasilich [John William], and with their help, we had it good. They were always concerned about us... They helped us so much, Ivan Vasilich and Vera, we really did not know how to thank them enough. Dear children, don't ever forget them, because on our arrival they helped us tremendously (p. 76).

Vera & John wedding. "My children, don't ever forget them."

Physically, Dad had been doing well, still farming his acres and showing no signs of sickness. But he was very lonely ever since Mom died in 1979. I have mentioned how he would show up at my door for an unannounced visit, indicating how lonely he was out on the farm by himself. My sisters, Lynda and Vera, helped him quite a bit in the years after Mom passed, coming over and washing his clothes and being company to him.

One day, about a month after John died, I called Dad and asked to have lunch with him. He came to my house, and that is when I advised him that we had some really bad news. I told him Reneé' was suffering from cancer and the doctors had given her less than a year to live. Father took the news hard. He made some comments about how it seemed like for so many years our family had happiness, and now so much tragedy was coming on us.

About a week after our lunch together, Father went to the funeral of a friend and gave the eulogy. As he walked out the door with brother Bill and a friend, on the steps of the church he collapsed from a heart attack and died right there. One second, he seemed fine, and the next second he was gone. It was like turning off a light switch. There was no suffering. My father died the way I want to die. Be healthy until the last day, then turn off the light switch and say good night.

I was at work at my Clovis store when I got the news about Dad. It hit me really hard, but I also knew he was now with the one he had loved for fifty years. I was not able to grieve for him the way I did for Mother, because at home I had my young wife lying in our bedroom, and every day I was watching her life slowly slip away. It was a rough time, but I did my best to encourage the boys and to keep my chin up at work.

After the funeral, because Father had a fairly large estate, my family was challenged with how all of that should be taken care of. Within our household growing up, especially among my brothers, we were raised to be fiercely competitive. That early conditioning was so strong that, after Father's death, there was much disagreement about who should control the distribution of the inheritance, even though our parents had left Lynda and Vera in charge of the trust. Sadly, the disagreements from those times have left tensions that remain to this day. But one thing we all have in common is that we loved our father, and we will always miss him.

My dad lived a hard life, but it was a good life. He grew up in a time of constant wars in Russia, frequently moving from one settlement to another, with his own father away for long periods. During most of those years he was raised by a stepmother who was harsh with him and did not send him to school or teach him how to read or write. After growing up and starting his own family, he was forced on two occasions to leave all of his hard-earned belongings behind and start penniless in a new country with a different language. But he never allowed hardships to become an excuse.

Father was born in 1907 and lived to the age of eighty. He was hard on us when we were young, but he became a nice, gentle person in his old age. He reminisced a lot with me about his youth, talking of how his father had a taxi service with a horse and wagon, and many other stories like that. He used to say, "Going back in time, son, it's like trying to bite your elbow. It's so close, but so far away." I have used that saying many times when talking with my kids and employees, emphasizing the lesson: Learn what you can today.

A few years before my father died, I gave him a cassette recorder and showed him how to use it. I also gave him some blank tapes and said, "Dad, you should record your memories." He did that, and throughout this book I have quoted from Father's Memoirs, which my sister Lynda transcribed and translated from the Russian. Dad has been gone more than thirty years now, but from time to time I still pull out one of those tapes and listen to his voice. When all is said and done, the big hero in my life is my dad. Had he not sacrificed and done all that he did, I would not be where I am.

In Iran, 1948

Shubin brothers and sisters (c. 1970)

The Five Shubin brothers (c. 1970)

Scott with Carlos Beccar in back, me, Reneé', Craig and Danny in front.

CHAPTER EIGHTEEN
LOSING RENEÉ

Reneé and I on a cruise

Reneé and I were a team, doing almost everything together. Sometimes people called us *The Beaver Family*, saying we were a lot like the family in that old show. I was Pop, working all day while, Mom was busy with the kids. Then Pop would come home, sit in his chair to read the paper and watch the news, while Mom fixed dinner and the kids were playing. Every year around Christmas it was like Santa Claus's sleigh broke down in front of our house and we helped him unload it! Along with all the gifts and decorations, a family in Tulare taught us how to make candy canes and peanut brittle, so every year at Christmas we had a big, candy-making party. We invited twenty or thirty couples with their children, and when people came for the first time, they would ask us, "How do you make candy canes?" I would tell them, "Just bring a paint brush, and we will show you!" Each year we had fifty or sixty people piled into our house, with everybody busy making candy canes and eating the catered food. In 1987, even with Reneé fighting the cancer, we still held our annual candy-making party, and everyone had a great time.

After each weekly chemo treatment, Reneé would be down for a couple days, and then she would rebound so strongly that it seemed there was really nothing wrong with her. I would get my hopes up, but then after a while I would see her getting weak again. It was quite an emotional roller coaster for all of us.

One day at the clinic in the early part of May, the doctor told us with a big smile that he had some great news. We listened with our own big smiles as he explained how Reneé's cancer was in 90% remission, and that she would not need any more chemotherapy! It seemed we had received our miracle, and I could not even describe the relief and happiness we felt. Reneé's first response was to tell the doctor that she and I had a tradition of snow-skiing, and she asked if she was in good enough shape for that? (Even though we were in May, the winter had been long and there was still enough snow on some of the peaks for the lifts to stay open.) The doctor told her, "Let's wait till I get the results of a bone marrow test that I'm scheduling for you on Friday." That was two days away, so on Thursday we started gathering things we would need for a snow-skiing vacation. The boys were excited, and it was a real happy time for us.

Friday came, and I took my wife in for her appointment. After the bone-marrow procedure, she was still heavily sedated, and the doctor told me she would probably sleep the rest of the day. I took her home where she got into bed. Reneé slept all through the day, and then all through the night. In the morning, I could not wake her up. I tried calling the doctor, but he was nowhere to be found. This was Saturday, one day before Mother's Day. Instead of making plans for taking my wife to a nice restaurant and showering her with gifts, I rushed her to the emergency room at St. Agnes Hospital.

The doctors examined Reneé and immediately ordered a blood transfusion. After that, she stayed in Intensive Care for two days, but there was no improvement. On the third day, the doctors moved her to a private room where she never woke up. Ten days later, on May 18, Reneé died.

Losing my wife rocked my world. I woke up one day and my best friend was not there anymore. In the days and months after that, sometimes at home as I sat in a chair watching the news or reading a paper, suddenly I would look toward the door, thinking Reneé was walking in. This happened a lot. As I mentioned before, I felt like God was punishing me. He had given me my best friend at a young age, and after living together in happiness for twenty years, He took her away. I think I was a good husband and a good father during those years, but I had my habits. I used to drink three or four beers before coming home from work, so instead of being there on time for a Little League game or a water polo match, I would show up late. I never cheated on Reneé, but I felt that I took her for granted, and that I could have done better. Everyone has their own way of processing tragedy, and I was doing my best to pull my world back together and move forward.

Reneé had a good life, but not without serious difficulties. She came from a broken home in Fresno where her dad was not around and her loving mother worked full time in Kerman, about twenty miles away. When Reneé came to Los Angeles to be close to me, her father allowed her to stay with him and his wife, but he did not intervene when the wife got drunk and mistreated his daughter. This painful experience seems to have been on Reneé's mind when she said to me, not long before she died, "Peter, you are still young, and some day you will remarry. Whoever you marry, be sure she is good to my kids."

Along with the pain of missing Reneé, I had three boys to raise, with the challenge of being both a father and a mother. I barely knew how to use a garbage disposal, and I knew nothing about washing clothes or using a dryer or a dishwasher. But we made it work. We did what we had to do.

The burial for Reneé was after a service at Clovis E.V. Evangelical Free Church. It was one of the largest funerals I have ever seen. On our way to the cemetery in our van, I remember looking in my rearview mirror and watching a line of cars following us from as far back as I could see.

Reneé missed Scott's high school graduation by about a month, but she knew he was a candidate for an aquatic scholarship at Fresno State University, and that he would receive the All-American trophy in water polo. Like their mother, all of my boys were good swimmers, and Reneé was pleased with how they were doing in school and in sports. I believe she left this world very proud of all her sons, and confident that they would do good in life.

In some ways, I do not think the boys dealt very well with their mom's passing. I believe they thought at first that she was going away for a short while and would be coming back. I spent as much time with them as I was able, but we were having big financial problems at the office, and I could not just walk away from my family's source of income. I spent the most time with Danny, who was still so young. He would get in bed with me at night, and I would put my arms around him and say, "Everything's gonna be alright." If I could go back, I would have gotten counseling for the boys, and I would have given more attention to what was going on inside of them. But I did my best at the time, as a 42-year-old father who had just lost the wife of his youth, and who needed to manage a household while running a complex business.

Another cruise

CHAPTER NINETEEN
LIFE AFTER RENEÉ

The Bureau of Automotive Repair had not let up in its crusade against me and my business. This process had been dragging on for years, and what finally helped turn the situation in my favor was the appointment of a new Bureau chief, Bill Good. Unlike the previous chief, Mr. Good had a history in the automotive repair business. My attorney, Dennis, made an appointment for us to go to Sacramento and meet with him. Once we got there, somehow it came out that Bill Good had learned to speak Russian, so we spent a little time letting him practice with me, and then we got down to business.

Dennis very professionally laid out all our complaints, one by one. We told Mr. Good that we were not doing anything different than anyone else, so we did not know why we were being harassed. We showed him documentation of how we had hired a Private Investigator to go into the Fresno Bureau office with phony complaints, and how Darrell Penner, the lead investigator, had a different policy for complaints that were made against *Goodguys*.

When the Bureau chief looked at all of this, he agreed to investigate the Fresno office. We were grateful to hear that, but we also wanted to see the documented results of the internal investigation. Since our company had been maliciously harassed by Bureau officials, I felt we had the right to see a copy of their investigation. Mr. Good told us he would not be able to turn over the results, but he did say that if we saw changes in the Fresno office, we would know they had found some wrongdoing.

About three months later, the head of the Bureau of Automotive Repair in Fresno, Yukio Tani, was retired. His assistant, Darrell Penner, got fired for sexual harassment. Those changes told me the Bureau had found wrongdoing. We ended up settling with the Attorney General's Office for twelve-month's probation (they had to come away with something!), and we agreed to not sue the State of California.

Those years of battling against the Bureau took a lot out of me. If there was ever a time when I felt I should just close up shop and head home, that was it. Not only was I fighting for survival in the business world, but in my private life I had gone through a series of major tragedies.

At the same time, that drawn-out experience with the Bureau taught me to be a better businessman, to pay more attention to detail and not leave myself open to bogus allegations. What still remained a mystery was WHY the Bureau had gone after my business in the way that they did? We knew about the complaint from the disgruntled employee, but that was not enough to explain why the Bureau put so much into the case.

About that time, because of our growth, we needed a mixing warehouse where we could bring in truckloads of tires. One day I was driving by an old building on G Street, and I noticed it was for lease. I called the number on the sign and spoke with a guy named Lou Markarian, telling him I needed a place for redistributing my products and starting a wholesale tire division. Lou and I agreed to meet the next day, and he showed me the building with its 16,000 square-foot warehouse and 4,000 square feet of office space. He said he wanted $3,000 a month for rent, so I asked how he would like to proceed. He told me I looked like an honest man, and that he would be satisfied with the first and last month's rent. I promptly gave him that, and he handed me the keys. Lou asked me to write the lease myself, so the next day I brought him a one-page, five-year lease, and we moved in. We stacked that old warehouse to the rafters with about 20,000 tires, and still had plenty of room left for our corporate office.

In August of 1989, I went to a 25-year class reunion where I ran into a gal I had a crush on in high school. She was a widow who worked as a Registered Nurse in Santa Monica. I do not know what got into me, but I jumped into a relationship with this woman, and a couple weeks after the reunion, she moved to Fresno and we eloped!

I had just wrapped up all that mess with the Bureau, and it seemed I was finally done with the difficult years that had lasted through the second half of the 1980s. It was time to enjoy something new!

Things started out well, but it did not take long for the situation to turn negative. I found out that the woman was in debt up to her ears, and then I learned that I had never known her when she was sober! What got me suspicious about the drinking was how she was always sipping from a glass of orange juice. At first, I thought she must really like orange juice, but after a while I started wondering what was in that glass. I waited for an opportunity to take a sip from it, but she was too sneaky. When she had a glass of water or something else, she would leave it sitting anywhere while she moved around the house. But with that orange juice, she always kept it with her, and I could never get close enough to see what was in it. That little cat-and-mouse game went on for a while, until I came up with a plan. One day I went to a grocery store and bought two bottles of Smirnoff. When I got home, I put those bottles in my bar, then I waited to see how long they would last.

Day after day went by, and to my surprise, those bottles stayed full. After a month, on a sleepless night at about three in the morning, I was tossing and turning when suddenly I got the idea to go check those bottles of vodka. I climbed out of bed and went down to the bar. On careful inspection, I saw that she had taken a razor blade and cut the seals, and after drinking all the vodka, she had filled the bottles with water!

After that, I learned she drank a quart of vodka every day. What she would do is raise her alcohol level to a range she liked to stay in, and whenever it fell below that level, her whole personality would change. But whether her level was high or low, she and I had an argument every single day. It was terrible beyond words.

The woman also did not get along with my boys, and they wanted her out of the house. One day Scott came to me and said he wanted to transfer his college enrollment from Fresno to Los Angeles. He did not tell me the reason, but I believed a big part of his decision was that things had become so miserable in the house that Scott wanted to get away. I told him I would support his decision, and also that he could take my El Camino. For the first time, one of my kids would be leaving home.

The day came, and as I was helping Scott pack his stuff in the car, I started crying. I do not cry often, but it really hurt to see my son leaving. In a very short time, we had gone from being a Leave It to Beaver family, to becoming one of the worst in the neighborhood. Reneé's words in her final days were haunting me. She had said, "Whoever you marry, make sure she's good to my kids." Well, I could make myself put up with the drinking, the daily arguments, and just about anything else, but this woman was not good to my sons, so she had to go.

I told her I was going to start the process for a divorce. She glared at me and told me very firmly that she would not agree to it. Why should she, with me paying all her bills so she could stay at home and drink all day? The process took some time, but finally my attorney had things ready for serving the divorce papers. Well, each time he sent someone to our door with the papers, the woman would not open the door!

Meanwhile, Scott had been enjoying his life in Los Angeles, but he never got around to attending school. I was okay with that, because after all he had been through, I wanted him to just have a good time for a while. After a few months, he came back to Fresno to heal from a knee surgery. Then, he decided he did not want to go back to L.A., and he asked if he could work for me. It was nice to have him back, and one day I said to him, "Hey, Scott, this woman keeps dodging the servers, so how about you serving her the divorce papers?" I did not have to twist his arm. My son could not wait to get home and hand her the papers.

When Scott got home, he saw the woman walking out to the mailbox. He stopped his car, got out, walked up to her and said, "I've got something for you." He tried to hand her the papers, but she knew what they were, and she refused to take them. Scott was determined to not leave without doing his job. He dropped the papers on the ground right in front of her and said, "You've been served." He got back in his car and drove back to tell me, "It's done."

Later that day, when I came home from work, she was madder than a wet hen. Boy, if I could have recorded some of the things she said to me! But it was done. My son had accomplished what the professional servers could not.

Over the next year, I got a first-hand taste of California divorce laws and how terrible a divorce-court battle can be. The woman clawed for every penny she could get, and when it was all over, that ten-month marriage cost me more than a hundred-thousand dollars. About five years later, one day I saw her picture in the obituary section of the newspaper. What a sad story, from start to finish.

That was a chapter in my life that I felt embarrassed and ashamed about, and I swore I would never marry again. After the divorce, I put my house up for sale. Although I had many beautiful memories from my history there, the last year was so terrible that I wanted to move. The house quickly sold, and I rented a place in Fresno. Then, I started looking for a piece of property to build a new house and make a fresh start.

One day in 1991 I was driving around Woodward Lakes at North Point in Fresno, looking for a home for sale or a place where I could build one. I spotted a vacant lot with a FOR SALE sign. Later that day, I called the number listed on the sign. A man answered and introduced himself as "Randy." We had a good talk. He told me the size of the lot and what he wanted for it. He also told me he was a custom home builder, and that I could get a discount on the lot if I hired him to build my house. We agreed to meet that same evening at the Red Robin restaurant in Clovis.

Randy and I hit it off from the start. After a few drinks, we agreed on the price for the lot, and also that Randy would build the home. I told him about a house that I liked and wanted to copy, with only some minor changes. The next day I drove with Randy and his designer to that location, and they drew a detailed copy of the house to be built on my lot.

Randy got busy filing all the necessary paperwork with the city, and soon after that, the construction started. In the meantime, he and I became the best of friends. His wife, Marilyn, helped me pick most of the tile and the colors, and the three of us started a tradition of going out to dinner on Thursday nights at the Limelight

Restaurant for Lobster Night. But something even bigger would soon come through my friendship with Randy.

Woodward Lake home

CHAPTER TWENTY
MANAGEMENT AGREEMENT PROGRAM

In August of 1992 I started my Management Agreement Program, which parallels a franchising program. I had an employee named John Brownrigg, who had been telling me he wanted to go into business for himself. In my experience, I have found that a lot of people go into business with great ideas and strong commitment, but they do not have a foundation from which to operate. They have no system for tracking sales, inventory, or accounts receivable. They do not realize the need for some sort of effective sales analysis to know what their store did on that day, or a profit and loss statement to know if they made a profit for that month, or a good way of accounting for doing year-end tax returns. They may have experience at being a good mechanic or salesman, but they do not know the legal ramifications of how to do a payroll, or how to handle human relations, or how to manage the technical requirements for running a business. All of this, and more, is involved in managing a complete tire and auto repair center, and many good people fail in their business because they do not have this foundation in place.

I wanted to start a program that provides all these things for people who want to have their own business. I spoke with my attorney, Rich Myers, and told him my idea about starting a franchising program. Rich assured me he was qualified to write such a program, and that he would do it for $5,000. Well, Rich kept coming back to me with stories about running into one legal hurdle after another. When he had milked me for $20,000, he told me that a franchising program would not work for me because of the cost and the red tape. He suggested I start what is called a *Management Agreement Program,* which is basically the same thing, but without the need for costly and burdensome legal obligations like an annual, audited financial statement for the State of California. So that is what I did.

My business partner, Tim, did not give much support in this. Tim never showed an interest in helping me, or in helping anybody who I felt was a qualified candidate for the program. But finally, it was all in place. On August 1, 1992, I put John Brownrigg into business under the Management Agreement Program, providing him and future franchisees with a complete administrative system.

My franchisees form their own corporation, and they operate with what is called a DBA (Doing Business As), meaning they have a licensing agreement with me to use my trademark name, *Goodguys Tire and Auto Repair.* This is a huge advantage for them, because in our industry a big part of success is name recognition. People remember names like Bridgestone, Firestone, Goodyear, Michelin, Hankook, and General. But here in this town, the name *Goodguys Tire and Auto Repair* is more recognized than all of them.

The program explains to my franchisees how their stores are going to look, and how they will support the programs we have built. We tell them that, first, we are going to sell tires; second, we are going to do what I call the intermediate part of the business;

and third, we are going to do auto repair. In all of this, I provide them with an accounting system, but I control everything within that system. This way, my franchisees cannot go in and change too much, which means they do not have the latitude to get themselves into trouble. We do their advertising, and we do all of their human relations like background checks on job applicants (something I did not do enough of in my early years). The program I provide is the only one like it in the Fresno area, and it has worked out well for my franchisees and also for me.

During the time that I was setting things up to start the program, I was taken by surprise when someone informed me of a secret deal that Goodyear's district manager, Rich Gibbons, was negotiating with one of my competitors. Gibbons was talking with another dealer about taking over my store on Blackstone and Dakota when the lease ran out. This was a store I had taken off their hands and turned into a successful business after they had lost money on it. When I heard about the plan to move me out of that location, I called the landowner, Sam Arnold, and asked if he might be interested in selling the property. He said it was funny that I would ask, because he had tried to contact Goodyear, but they were not returning his calls. I asked Mr. Arnold what his intentions with the property were, and he told me he was at the age where he preferred to sell it. He said he wanted $350,000, with $50,000 down and interest for ten years, and then to be cashed out. I said, "Great! What do we do now?" He said if we go to the escrow company and open a thirty-day escrow, I could have it in a month.

After purchasing the property that Goodyear was secretly negotiating to sub-lease to my competitor, I sent a letter to Rich Gibbons, informing him that I was their new landlord and that Goodyear should kindly remit their future rent payments to 925

Clovis Avenue, ATTN: Peter M. Shubin. I also said there was an underground oil tank which Goodyear had installed without landlord approval, and would they kindly remove it. I would have loved to be a fly on the wall in Gibbons' office when he read that letter!

About a year later, the Goodyear rep called me one day and asked if I was interested in their vacant stores on Shaw and Fresno, Blackstone and Herndon (a brand new store that had not yet been opened), and Shaw and Brawley (still under construction). I told him I would lease all three if Goodyear would let me out of my lease on the store at Fulton Mall. I also asked that Goodyear pay for the sales fixtures and equipment in the three stores, and that I get six months of free rent, with all of this on a ten-year lease. They reported my request to Akron, and it was quickly approved.

Meanwhile, the new house in Fresno was steadily taking shape. Basically, I had it designed as a bachelor's pad, figuring no one else would ever live there except me and the boys. But just in case a woman ever did come to live with me, Marilyn picked out pink tiles for the main shower, and a few other touches of color that a woman might like. That was just in case.

CHAPTER TWENTY-ONE
CHARLESIA

One afternoon in September of 1993, I went to a tailgate party at a Fresno State football game. There were about eight couples in our group, with me as the only single person. I was busy cooking up shish kebabs when I noticed Randy talking with a friend of his named Jeff, who had written the fire insurance policy for my house. A few minutes later, Jeff walked up to me and said, "Pete, you're single, aren't you?" I jokingly said, "Hey, Jeff, back off." He shook his head and said, "Pete, I got this friend, and she's a neat person. You really gotta meet her!" I said, "Jeff, I just went through a terrible divorce, and I don't want anything to do with another woman." I thought that would settle it, but Jeff held his eyes on mine and said, "Pete, you gotta meet this girl." I laughed, and then I told him, "Jeff, I got my preferences." I ran off a short list of what I preferred in a woman, including her being "about my age but not looking it." I said, "If she's got all that, I'm willing to meet her." Jeff smiled and said, "Pete, she's got all that."

He told me her name is *Charlesia*, but when I could not pronounce it, he said to just call her *Charly*. I said, "Alright, I'll call her Charly." He gave me her phone number, and a couple days later I worked up the courage to call. Charlesia and I talked a few minutes, and we agreed to meet at the Peppermill Restaurant in

Fresno. She said she would come there straight from work and would be wearing a dress. I told her I would be wearing shorts.

The day came. It was the third Thursday of September. I went to the Peppermill, and after sitting at the bar a few minutes, I saw a beautiful lady in shorts walk in and take a seat three chairs away. I could see her in the mirror and could not keep from admiring her. I started hoping the lady in the dress would not show up, because this lady in shorts was beautiful and maybe I could start up a conversation! Well, a few more minutes passed, and we kept stealing glances at each other. Finally, she turned to me and said, "Are you Peter?" I said, "Yeah." She said, "I'm Charlesia." I noticed right away that Jeff had not been exaggerating when he told me, "Pete, she has all that." Charlesia and I stayed until closing time at midnight, and the conversation went so well that we decided to have dinner again.

Charlesia (c. 1993)

The next night we went to Nicolas Restaurant, and once again we really enjoyed our time together. On the way home we decided to buy a bottle of wine, the kind she likes, and we went to the apartment she shared with her daughter, Wendy, and her grandson, Nick.

Wendy and Nick were not there, so Charlesia and I had a quiet time alone. At the end of the night I asked her what she was going to do for the weekend. She said she was going to the Bay Area, and then she asked what I was going to do. I said I did not have any plans, but that I was thinking she and I could go to Bass Lake. I started telling her how nice that place is, not knowing she had planned to go to the Bay Area to see her ex-husband. When I invited Charlesia to come with me to Bass Lake, she had to make the biggest decision of her life, to either go back and try again at an old relationship, or stay and start a new one. She chose to go with me.

We went to Bass Lake and had a great weekend. On our way back we stopped at a pub, and as we sat at the bar, I looked at her and said, "You know, as much as I hate to say so, I think I'm falling in love with you." She looked at me, and with a twinkle in her eye, she said, "Spell my first name." Out of all the things to say! I could not even pronounce her name, much less spell it. But I was on the spot, so I did my best, but I got it wrong. Then she leaned a little closer and said, "I think I'm falling in love with you, too." I had been feeling embarrassed for misspelling her name, but now the only thing I felt were goose bumps.

For the next three or four weeks, we got together each night for drinks and dinner. I met her oldest daughter, Wendy, who was very nice. I saw that Wendy worked hard to take care of her son, Nick, a fine young boy who was already showing signs of being a great musician on the piano and the guitar.

One night in October I said to Charlesia, "We've been going out so much, and we've fallen in love with each other, but can you cook?" She looked at me and said, "Of course I can cook!" I told her that Craig's birthday was on October 22, a few days away. She told me she would be there to make dinner for the occasion. When the day came, Charlesia put in hours getting the food ready. I came home from work and saw that she had cooked enough for what looked like fifty people. I said, "Charly, this is just going to be for about ten people!" She shrugged and said, "Well, there will be plenty for everybody." She made an Italian dinner that was probably the best I ever had, with all the hors d'oeuvre, martinis and everything. She was showing herself to be all that I could want or dream about in a wife.

By early November, the house was ready. Some of the things I love the most about it are the very high ceilings and the wide hallways (four-feet wide, rather than the standard three). As I mentioned, although it was built with the idea of being a bachelor's pad, Marilyn had the pink tiles installed just in case a woman ever came to live with me. Well, wouldn't you know it, Charlesia came to live with me, and she does not like the pink tiles! But, pink tiles and all, she and I moved into the house together on November 4, 1993.

On the same day we moved in, Charlesia's mom and dad came by to meet me for the first time. They wanted to see what their daughter was getting herself into! Her parents' names were Charolene and Oscar Thomas, but we always called them Oma and Opa (German for Grandma and Grandpa). They had adopted Charlesia as an infant and lovingly raised her, and they were really the nicest people I could ever have met. They were Christians who took their faith seriously and had brought their daughter with them to church several times each week while she was growing up. Oma and Opa accepted me as family from the day I met them.

About a month after moving into the house, we flew to Oregon for a weekend with Charlesia's younger daughter, Heather, who had two children (Charlesia, and Riley the newborn). Heather had another son, Douglas, who had been adopted out at birth. It was an open adoption, so that Doug always knew who his birth mother was. I saw that Heather was a real nice lady, and she seemed very happy for her mom. She gave her blessing to our relationship, and after a few days with them, we headed home.

A couple weeks later we drove to Santa Rosa to see Charlesia's Aunt Rena, with whom she had always been very close. Rena was engaged to a real nice man named Bill Cotton. Rena and Bill lived for five o'clock at night. That was martini time. They would only have one martini, plus a little bonus. We had a good time with them, and I enjoyed my time with Charlesia everywhere we went. We had the same feelings for each other, and we believed that we were meant to be. I knew without a doubt that God was looking after me by sending me this lady.

On Christmas Eve I asked Charlesia to marry me, and she accepted. I bought a beautiful diamond ring and put it on her finger. We decided to have a private wedding with just the two of us, so we found a nice little chapel in Pacific Grove, a place she loved and had often visited. On February 26, 1994, we drove to Pacific Grove and made our vows. That night we had a fine wedding-night dinner at a restaurant called The Sardine Factory on Cannery Row. I felt, as I still do and always will, that God had blessed me and forgiven me for my failures, by giving me a wife who is the kindest, nicest, and most beautiful woman any man could ever meet.

We took a week off for our honeymoon and traveled up the California coast. After a night at the Monterey Plaza Hotel, we drove to Bodega Bay and stayed there two days. From there we drove about a hundred miles north to Mendecino and checked into the Little River Inn, which had a nine-hole golf course. Charly told me she was going to sleep in the next morning, so I said, "I'm gonna go out and hit some golf balls in the morning." I got up early and went out on the uphill course, and I saw fog that was different than any I had ever seen. The fog I am used to just sits on the ground and you can't see anything else, but in that area, it sits higher in the air. As I stood on the grass in the early morning and looked up the hill along the course, I could see the fog like a low cloud about a hundred feet above the ground. I just stood there for a while in amazement.

From Mendecino, we headed further north and spent a night at the Bimbo Inn, one of the oldest hotels in Northern California. After that we drove a little further to where Highway 101 connects with Highway 1. We caught the 101 and ventured back to Santa Rosa, where we spent a night with her Aunt Rena, who invited Bill to come over and have a martini with us. We had a good time with them, and the next morning we headed home, happy and looking forward to the rest of our lives together.

After the beautiful honeymoon, we decided to have a wedding reception at our house. We invited all her friends and mine, along with a couple family members. Everybody loved Charlesia, and I was the happiest husband there ever was.

I am very content in my life with my wife. She is good to my kids, who love and respect her. I am good to her kids, too. I try to help them when there is a need, and they seem to have a lot of respect for me. We try to celebrate our holidays and the many birthdays together, but since her children are all in Oregon (Wendy moved there in 1996), it makes it difficult.

I would like to close this chapter by saying to Charlesia,

> *Behind every successful man is a strong woman. I want to thank you for going through a lot of ups and downs with me and having faith in me, that together we would succeed both in family and in business.*

CHAPTER TWENTY-TWO
A NEW VENTURE

One day in July of 1994, I was with my outside salesman and we called on a young dealer in Sanger, about twenty miles southeast of Fresno. Goodyear had put him in there, even though he did not know anything about the tire and auto repair business. He told me he really wanted to get out, and he asked if I would like to buy his store. I asked what he wanted for it, and he said, "I owe about $11,000 on some equipment that I bought, so if you'll just take over the payments on this piece of equipment, you can take over the lease for that." I agreed right there, and in thirty days we took over that store. We cleaned it up, painted it, refurbished it, and identified it with my logo.

Sanger store

About that time, I went to see my doctor for an annual check-up. After getting the results of my lab tests, he told me I was a "borderline diabetic." The doctor prescribed pills to take each day, and I did that, but he also prescribed a healthier diet and more exercise, which I did not do. I was living too fast to slow down and really think that if I did not make some changes, I would eventually become a full-blown diabetic.

Later that same year I stumbled onto something that made me a lot of money. It started when I needed a battery for my brick telephone. Wherever I went in search of a battery, I was told my type of phone was discontinued and I would have a hard time finding what I needed. Well, one day at a Motorola store I happened to grab an industry magazine, and as I was browsing through it, I read about a guy in Kansas City who refurbished telephones and sold them. His name was Mark, so I called and told him what I needed. He assured me that he would send the battery, and then we just started talking about things in the business. After a while, Mark said to me, "Hey dude, I want to open your eyes to something." He started telling me about something called a bundling law, and he suggested that I become a ConTel Cellular dealer in California.

Well, I did not know what he was talking about, but he went on to explain that California had a law which said you could not give somebody something and expect them to sign up for service *unless* the stuff you were giving them was refurbished, reconditioned, discontinued and no longer made. What this meant is that a company like ConTel Cellular could not give a new phone to someone and then require that person to also sign up for phone service. So, what Mark ran down to me was an idea for how I could make a lot of money by signing up customers for service with ConTel. He said, "California is a gold mine for this, and most people don't know it."

I was all ears as Mark told me he could sell me refurbished phones for $50 each, and I could give them away free to everyone who buys a set of tires. Then, I could say to the customer, "What are you going to do with the phone?" Well, of course the customer would need *service* for the phone, and at that point I would offer to sign the person up for service with ConTel, who would pay me $200-$300 for every customer I signed up (depending on what program the customer signed up for). I told Mark, "You gotta be kidding me." He said, "No dude, I'm not kidding you. What you need to do is get ahold of ConTel Cellular and tell them you want to become a dealer. You take out a full-page newspaper ad, put a picture of a bag phone in the center of the ad, and say, 'Free cell phone with the purchase of four tires.'" He told me, "Dude, your tire sales will skyrocket, and you'll make a ton of money signing up customers for ConTel."

This was one of those times in my life that leads me to believe I have a Guardian Angel. On that very same day, after talking with the guy from Kansas, I was pulling out of a parking lot at one of my stores and I saw Carlos Beccar, the foreign-exchange student who had stayed with us a few years earlier and who still called me "Dad." He had stopped by the store just to visit me. We parked and started talking, just getting caught up on what was going on with each other. When I told him about the idea with the cellphone service, his eyes lit up. Wouldn't you know it, Carlos was working for ConTel! He said to me, "Dad, that would be a great deal." I immediately said, "Well, let me ask you a question. Will you quit your job and work for me and run this portion of the business?" He said, "Yeah, I'll do that."

We did not waste time. I called ConTel and told them about the business I run and what I wanted to do with the phones. I was talking to a gal named Kathy, and she said, "We'd love to sign you on as a dealer." I asked her if ConTel would contribute to an advertising campaign, and she said she would talk with her supervisor. A little later she called me back and said that ConTel would give me $5,000 in advertising funds to kick it off. I quickly got together with Carlos and we ordered a hundred phones from Mark. While we waited for the phones to arrive, we put a large ad in the Fresno Bee, saying, "Free cell phone with the purchase of four tires." Boy did that idea take off.

We had nine or ten stores at the time, and after a customer bought a set of tires, our salesman would give him a coupon to take to Carlos, whom we had set up with a small office at one of our stores. When the customer showed the coupon, Carlos would hand him a bag phone and ask if he wanted to sign up for service. It worked like a charm, and my largest monthly commission check from ConTel was for more than $100,000. Things got so busy for Carlos that I hired Charlesia's daughter, Wendy, to work with him.

After a while, we had a problem with a nearby electronics company called *Goodguys Electronics*. Because I was advertising the giveaway of cell phones with the purchase of tires, people would see the name *Goodguys*, and they were calling *Goodguys Electronics* to ask about the free cell phones! The electronics company finally got tired of hearing it, and they decided to sue me for trademark infringement. We went to court, and we found out that their trademark covered electronics, but not cell phones, which at that time was still a new industry. Our trademark covered tires and auto repair but did not cover cell phones either. So, we agreed that we would stop giving away phones, and I formed another company and called it CellMart. That is how I was able to keep the very profitable business going with ConTel.

In the eighteen months of working with ConTel, our average monthly commission was about $35,000. It finally ended when

California lifted the bundling law, which quickly dried up our little business. When it was over, I did not have to swallow any overhead losses, because there had been no overhead to begin with. I walked away with about a half-million-dollar profit, Carlos went back to his job with ConTel, and Wendy moved to Oregon where she later got married.

The cell phone deal ended in 1996, and several years had now passed since we wrapped up that mess with the Bureau. Even though that ordeal was behind us, the mystery still remained as to *why* there was ever such a problem at all? Well, one day it so happened that I put out a newspaper ad for a salesman. A day or two later, my general manager called and said, "Pete, you'll never believe who wants to come in and interview for that job." I said, "Who?" He told me, "Darrell Penner." I said, "You gotta be kidding me!" He assured me that he was not kidding, and he asked if I wanted him to do the interview. I said, "No, I want to personally do this one." Next thing I knew, this guy who had tried to run me out of the automotive business was sitting in my office asking for a job. That was the longest job interview I ever did. It lasted five hours.

Penner looked like a wet rat, sitting in that chair and trying to disguise his embarrassment. After telling me his wife had divorced him, he spilled his guts on the whole story about me being harassed by the Bureau. It had started with the former employee, Chris Arnold, whom we fired from our Weber store for stealing. Arnold wrote a letter claiming that my company trains its salespeople how to cheat and scam customers. He gave the letter to his mother, who worked across the hall from Penner. I do not know what Arnold's mother might have had on Penner, but he was eager to do what she wanted with the letter she hand-carried to his office. He had Arnold sign a document, stating under penalty of perjury that everything he wrote in his letter was true. Penner then proudly took it to Sacramento and got some attaboys from the Bureau Chief and from Arnold's mother.

Penner told me the Bureau Chief at that time (the one whom Bill Good replaced) was putting pressure on all the Bureau offices to do more to accumulate consumer complaints. So, when Penner read the letter with Arnold's complaints, it seemed perfect for what the guys up in Sacramento wanted to see. He told me the Bureau had really wanted to go after Goodyear Tire on a statewide basis, but instead they settled for me. In those early days we were still advertising under the name *Goodyear Tire Centers*, so the Bureau was thinking that when this story hits the media, the Goodyear signs would be on display and the public would think Goodyear was in hot water for cheating their customers. The Bureau did not want to take on Goodyear directly because of the money it would cost. Since I looked and acted like Goodyear, but did not have their financial resources, the Bureau jumped on the opportunity to come after me.

It seems that Penner's world fell apart after Chief Good ordered the internal investigation. His wife divorced him, he lost his job, and now he was coming to me in hope of a hire. He told me that if I decided to sue the State, he would testify on my behalf and reveal all the scams the Bureau had pressured him and other consumer-complaint investigators to do. I thought Penner might be good to have around, just in case we had any other problems with the Bureau, so I asked him to write a job description to help us see where he would best fit in with our organization. He never came back, and the last I heard, he was working in a little garage that occasionally brings to my store on West Shaw alignment jobs that his store is not able to do.

That interview with Penner brought something of a closure to what had been quite a story. Overall, I had to spend about a quarter-million dollars in legal costs, not to mention the income lost when our business dropped during the bad publicity. I am still amazed at how one person acting recklessly can cause so many problems for others.

CHAPTER TWENTY-THREE
SOME VACATIONS WITH CHARLESIA

One of the things Charlesia and I both love is to travel. Our first vacation was to the Fiji Islands, and then on to Australia, about a year after we married. Before arriving at the islands, I had not realized there are people who still live in huts, with no access to television or other technologies that we take for granted. I found out that the Fijians are basically self-supporting, and the only need they have for imports is coffee, tea and sugar. Everything else they get on their own, like fish and meat. They do not drink alcohol, but they have a custom of drinking what they call Kava, which looks like muddy water and tastes like a root. Whereas we have bartenders, they have a *kavatender*. Their drink is different than alcohol, which takes you up after a couple of drinks, and then after a couple more it depresses you. Kava does not take you up, it just brings you straight down! In one of their places of business, I walked up to the kavatender, but he was asleep from all the kava he had drank. One of the natives said to me, "You have to clap twice to wake him up." I guess that was their custom, so I did it, and sure enough after the second clap, the man got up and poured me a cup. It slightly numbed my tongue and lips, and while I was drinking it, the kavatender went back to sleep. When I finished, I did the same thing, and on the second clap he stood and poured me another cup. Charlesia and I got a good laugh from that.

The Fijian natives also made nice music with their somewhat primitive instruments, and they loved to dance. One time when we were standing around, a native lady walked up to me, grabbed me, and started dancing me all over the floor. While that was going on, a native man grabbed my wife and did the same with her. I do not want to say this in an insulting way, but their hygiene standards are different than ours, and the natives who danced with us had a very strong odor. You should have seen the look on Charlesia's face as she danced with her head pulled back to get away from the smell. Their body odor was so strong that when we got to our room, Charlesia bagged up our clothes and threw them away. But it was fun, and I could see she was having a good time.

One day our ship captain took us to a beautiful bay, but even more stunning than the bay was Charlesia in her blue, one-piece bathing suit. We both went out for a swim, but she went a lot farther than I wanted to go, so I swam back to the sand to wait for her. A few minutes later she shouted to me, "Peter, I've got a shark following me!" I yelled for her to "paddle real steady and head straight this way." She was about a hundred yards out, and as she swam to shore, that shark trailed her most of the way. When she came out of the water and stood on the sand, I was so struck by her beauty that I could not blame that shark for wanting to follow her!

One day on a cruise we stopped at a certain island where the guys from another ship challenged us to a volleyball game on the beach. I had brought a case of baseball caps with a *Goodguys Tire and Auto Repair* logo, to give away as gifts. Before the match, I gave each guy on our ship one of those brand-new hats. They were so proud to wear them, like they were wearing uniforms. I guess because I had given away the hats, they picked me as the team captain. I got them all organized and pumped up for the match, but when we went out to play, I had drunk so much that I fell asleep. My guys played hard and won, with their captain snoring on the sand! We really had fun during our time in Fiji, and Charlesia told me she looked forward to going there again.

From Fiji we flew to Australia, where my wife hurt her back and had to spend a lot of time in bed for the rest of the vacation. We still made the best of it, and Charlesia was able to accompany me at my niece, Karen's, wedding. That was our main reason for going to Australia. A lot of work had gone into planning the wedding, and it was a beautiful event with about two-hundred people. After that, we went to a celebration at the local casino. My sister Annie (Karen's mom) and her husband Mike owned a manufacturing company that made furniture for the casino, so they were able to get us all rooms, and we had a great time.

One day Annie let me use her car, and her son Matt and I went out for a long drive, with me behind the wheel. That was my first experience driving from the right seat of a car along what felt like the wrong side of the road! I kept weaving over to the right side, where I was used to driving, because it felt so awkward to drive on the left. At one point, Matt said, "Uncle Pete, would you like me to drive?" I said, "No, I'll make it." My nephew stayed very alert and kept me on the left side of the road the whole time.

Although Charlesia had the problem with her back, we really did have fun in Australia. When we got home, we felt refreshed and satisfied.

About five years later, we went back to Australia. One of the highlights on that second trip was a cross-country train ride that started from the most northwestern part of the country. Annie had chartered first-class train accommodations for us and the four others in our group, but shortly before we got on board, the company told her they did not have those accommodations available. When Annie insisted that they do something, they agreed to hook up the car that was used by Australia's Ambassador, and to let us ride in that! We had our own chef and butler, and we slept in a king-sized bed.

The train dropped us off in a town called Alice Springs, where we stayed a few days and did some hiking and hill climbing. One night we rode camels through the desert for about an hour's distance until we came to a place where we had a beautiful barbeque dinner. To get on the camels, the tour guide brought us to something like a loading dock where we slung our legs over the animal between the humps. I will never forget the look on Charlesia's face when her camel started to move and she blurted out, "Oh, shoot!" But she got over that little scare, and we all had a fun time riding under the starry summer sky. When we went back to Alice Springs, instead of riding camels we took a bus, and during that ride we saw the most amazing thing. Going along the road at about fifty miles an hour, we looked out the window and saw camels running alongside of us!

From there we caught a plane to Sydney where we rode in a tour boat and saw the famous Sydney Bridge all lit up in the night. Boy was that a sight. At a little shop I bought a painting of the Sydney Harbor with its bridge, done by an artist named Peter Lik. The painting is about five feet wide and more than two feet long, and when you shine lights on it in just the right way, it gives the effect of the city lights coming on. Then, when you shift the lights, the city behind the bridge goes dark.

I also have a very unusual memory from that trip to Australia. We were in a restaurant, and one of the guys in our group left the table for the men's room. He came back laughing, like he had just seen something hilarious. I asked him what was so funny, but all he said was, "You gotta go try the men's room!" I told him, "I'm not going to do that. I don't have to go." But when dinner was over, I did have to go.

I left the table and walked to the men's room. Inside, it had a long urinal with a mirror above it. Anyone standing at the urinal could see themselves in the mirror. I stepped up and started to do what I had come there for. All of a sudden, something about the mirror changed, and I was looking directly at everyone in the restaurant. I could see them plain as day, sitting at their tables, like I was looking through a clear window. I could not believe the restaurant had designed its men's room so the people eating food at their tables could see into the men's urinal! I zipped it up quick and hurried out of there.

When I came flying out the door, the people at my table were doubled over, laughing. That is when I realized the window in front of the urinal was actually a one-way mirror. It was designed so that when the back of the urinal got wet, something about the lighting changed, and everyone out in the restaurant suddenly became visible. For those who did not already know, it was quite an experience, to suddenly think you are peeing right in front of people eating at their tables.

Those were some of the highlights of my wonderful, second trip to Australia with my wife, Charlesia.

CHAPTER TWENTY-FOUR
MORE VACATIONS WITH CHARLESIA

Over the years, my wife and I have taken trips to places like London, France, Spain, Mexico, Germany, Russia, Korea, and several times to the Caribbean. One trip that stands out in a humorous way is when Goodyear invited us, along with a group of other tire dealers, to Athens, Greece. After we boarded the plane, Charlesia took a sleeping pill and slept through the whole flight, while I went to the back and drank with my buddies. When we got to Athens and checked into the hotel, I guess from the combination of jet lag and all that alcohol at 30,000 feet, I laid down in our bed and slept for three nights and two days. Charlesia could not wake me up. I slept through our whole vacation! On the last day, when I finally woke up, I felt like I owed her for sleeping all that time. I asked the tour director if she could extend our trip and arrange a tour of the Greek islands. She agreed, and we extended our stay by five days. We toured the Aegean Sea and saw islands like San Sorini, one of the most beautiful I have ever seen.

In 2001 we had an amazing journey through several countries. My brother Bill and his wife accompanied us, along with several friends, including Daniel Bonyhadi, a wine exporter/importer from

Fresno. Our first stop was in Austria, where Daniel picked out a certain restaurant and said that he would treat. When I asked him how he knew about this place, he said he had been researching his genealogy, and he learned that his grandfather from Austria had a mistress whom he often brought to this restaurant. Daniel said he wanted to see what kind of taste his grandfather had. Well, the restaurant served us a ten-course meal, and each course was paired with a small glass of wine. There were no prices on the menus, but I did not care, because Daniel was paying for everything! When dinner was finally done, and we had ten glasses of wine in our bellies, the servers rolled out the dessert tray, which had everything from Cuban cigars to Austrian port wines.

From Austria we flew to St. Petersburg, Russia, where we spent a few days, toured all the museums and castles, and then caught a ship up the Volga River to Moscow. We started at sea level and passed through about a dozen locks. It was a memorable four-day journey in that 32-foot wide, 150-foot long riverboat. As we traveled, we noticed leaks in the walls of the locks, and in some places we saw rebar sticking out. When I asked the tour director about it, he told me they had built those locks in the 1700s, at a time when the Russian Czar, Peter the Great, wanted Russia to become more like a Western country. The Czar wanted the canal built on the European model, so when the Russian engineers started building the locks, they shipped in truckloads of cement, but the truck drivers would sell half the cement along the way and replace it with dirt. The locks ended up getting built with cement mixed with dirt, and that is why they came out looking so shabby. Charlesia and I got a good laugh out of that little story, trying to imagine those Russian truck drivers delivering dirt to the engineers, who thought they were getting pure cement to build a great canal for the Czar!

When we got to Moscow, we met up with my cousin Tanya, along with three other people who were friends of my brother Bill and his wife, Martha. I found it really terrible, the way the Russians treat their common people. Russia is a two-tier society, with the *haves* and the *have-nots*. Whereas the *haves* are noticed by their high-dollar dress, lipstick, perfume, etc., the *have-nots* are easily recognized by the clothes they wear, and by not using such things as perfume and lipstick. My cousin is a *have-not*, and on the first day we tried to take her and Bill's friends to a nice restaurant for lunch. The management told us they did not have enough food for our group of twelve, and they suggested we go to a certain restaurant around the corner. We went there, and it was about the worst lunch I ever had!

The next day we tried again to take everyone to a fancy restaurant, but the management would not let the locals in. I thought it was awful how they would show that kind of prejudice toward less-privileged people. But I was determined that my group was going to enjoy a good meal in a nice restaurant, so I bribed the maître d with a hundred-dollar bill, and we all went in. After we ate, the waitress handed us the bill on a three-foot-long strip of paper from one of those old adding machines. It was all in Russian, which I can speak but cannot read very well. I kept the bill in order to find out later what we had been charged for. When I got back to Fresno, I showed it to a friend named Margo who looked it over and said, "Wow, they charged you guys for every little thing, like butter, salt, pepper and napkins!"

From Moscow we boarded a large riverboat and sailed for a day, and after that we took a train to Berlin and toured both east and west. We saw the old place of Checkpoint Charlie, and we noticed how the western side had developed to look better than the east. When we were back on the train, I got a call from Scott. He said,

"Dad, did you hear what's going on over here?" I said, "No. What's going on?" He told me about the radicals flying airplanes into the Twin Towers. I hung up the phone and went immediately to the television where we saw it with our own eyes. We were shocked, in disbelief. At that point, we just wanted to get home, but after we took a ship across the Channel to a port outside of London, we saw that all the airlines were shut down. The only planes in the sky were military. We had our credit cards to get a hotel and anything else we needed, but we did not feel right about having a good time in Europe with all that tragedy happening at home. What had started out as a great vacation did not end so well.

One other trip that stands out in my life as I remember it, is the time we went to South Korea. It was in 2002, and Hankook Tire and Rubber Co. invited me to the World Cup Soccer finals in Seoul. We flew first class on Korean Airlines, and all the way there I was expecting to see a third-world country. Boy, was I surprised to see how wrong I was. Everywhere I went, I saw that the South Koreans are hard-working, highly motivated, and highly developed in business, technology, and service.

One day the Korean tour guide took us to a tire factory where they manufactured 80,000 tires a day and shipped them all over the world. I am not exaggerating when I say that only about a dozen employees worked in that huge factory. Nearly everything was automated and run by robots. I was impressed with the cleanliness and efficiency. I have been in Cooper Tire's manufacturing plant, and also Armstrong's, but this one in Korea was the cleanest and most sophisticated I have ever seen.

Charlesia and I had a really great time that day, but coming back on the tour bus, we got concerned because the driver was speeding. As we watched him, we realized he was about to fall asleep. We both got up and walked to the front where we stood right next to that driver and sang "God Bless America" very loudly all the way back to Seoul. That was how we kept him awake!

I do not remember much about the soccer match in Korea, but what does stand out is the day the tour director took us to the Demilitarized Zone (DMZ) between the South and the North. I was amazed to see Korean soldiers from each country standing about fifty yards apart, with their rifles pointed directly at each other! It seemed comical, and I had to remind myself that those are real guns with real bullets. But even more comical were the beautiful houses and buildings I saw through binoculars looking toward the North. At least, I *thought* they were beautiful houses and buildings. The tour guide explained that those structures are nothing more than facades which the North Korean government set up to give the *appearance* of great prosperity!

Another unusual experience from that trip was being escorted along the DMZ and seeing large, red, triangular objects alongside the road. At one point I said to the guide, "What are those red, triangular things?" She told me they are signs to warn of landmine areas. She explained how after the Korean War ended in 1953, the government offered an acre of land to anybody who would go in and clear out those mines. But nobody was ever willing to even try. I said to her, "You mean if I walked out into that area, there's a chance I could get blown up?" She said, "Yes." Needless to say, I did not go out there.

Those are some of my experiences with my wife in our vacation travels around the world. For me, nothing in life is better than just being with Charlesia, whether we are out somewhere traveling or just sitting around together at home.

CHAPTER TWENTY-FIVE
SELLING STORES

One day in April of 1997, I was out with my salesman and we called on a guy named Joe Hightower from Visalia, about seventy miles south of Fresno. When we tried to sell him some tires, he looked at me and said, "Hey, can I talk to you privately?" Joe and I went into a room where he told me he wanted out of the business. He asked if I would like to buy his store, so I asked what he wanted for it. He gave me a price that included the property, the inventory, and the equipment inside. I told him I would give some thought to his offer.

When I got back to Fresno, I asked my banker how good my credit was. She said that whatever I want, I could have, so I told her I was thinking about buying some property in Visalia. She said the bank would do an appraisal on the property, and that if everything checked out, they would finance me. A short time later, the loan was approved and I bought the store. But it turned out to be a bad decision. Visalia was too far away to manage a business from Fresno, and my Fresno guys did not want to drive that far or move there. After about three years we closed it up, since the property payment was cheaper than the cost of keeping the store open.

Shortly before purchasing the store in Visalia, I got a call from a man named Tim Lobb, who represented himself as the western-region retail manager for America's Tire Company (AKA: Discount Tire of Arizona). Lobb told me his company was thinking of expanding into the Fresno market, and they wanted to know if I was interested in selling my retail business? I told him I have given that some thought, and I would be interested in talking about it if the offer was right. Lobb scheduled a meeting with his company's owner, Bruce Halle, and we agreed to meet at the Peppermill Restaurant in Fresno. They brought their attorney, along with Bruce Halle's son, and I came with my partner Tim and our accountant, Ted Starkel.

The conversation at the Peppermill started with Bruce saying his company was interested in buying *some* of my stores. I told him this was a little different than what Tim Lobb had said to me on the phone, when he had told me they were interested in buying *all* of my stores. Bruce said they were not interested in all of them because some were in pretty bad areas. He told me they were only interested in Blackstone and Dakota, Shaw and Fresno, Clovis Avenue, and Clovis and Kings Canyon. I said, "Well, however many stores you buy, as long as the price is the same, it doesn't matter to me. One store would be the same price as ten. Two stores would be the same price as ten." Bruce thought about it a minute, and then he threw a price at me. I quickly said, "That sounds like it's a price for four stores. I have ten stores for sale." Bruce immediately doubled the offer, and I knew I could probably squeeze him a little more if I wanted to, but after discussing it briefly with Tim, we decided to take the offer.

The deal with Bruce and his company was going to be in cash, and they basically did not want us to leave anything in our stores. In other words, they were going to pay us a lot of money for empty stores. We were to take everything out of the locations so that America's Tire could start from scratch and refurbish each one according to their standard design for all their stores nationwide. I told them I also wanted it in the contract that half of the cash payment would be for the sale of the locations, and the other half would be for their company to hire Tim and I as artificial consultants. My reason for this was that if we had taken all the cash for the sale of the stores, half of it would have gone to the government. But under the contract, I was able to depreciate the payment over a ten-year period, and thereby save a lot of money in taxes. We put the stores into escrow, and America's Tire drew up an artificial consulting agreement. (I never heard from them on this, but on paper both Tim and I were hired by that company to be on call for business consultations.)

As I mentioned, one of the stores we sold to America's Tire was the location at Fresno and Shaw, but what I could not tell them was that Goodyear had recently notified me it was not going to renew its lease on that location. Goodyear had advised me that if I intended to stay there, I should get ahold of the landlord and negotiate my own lease. This meant I had only ninety days left before the lease on that location expired.

I called the landlord, a woman named Joan Kevorkian, and I asked if she had gotten a letter from Goodyear saying they would not exercise their lease option. She said that she had received the notice, and that she did not want a vacancy at that location. I negotiated with her for a ten-year lease, and I made sure the contract had a sublease provision. This meant I had the right to sublease the property with the landlord's consent, and that such consent would not be unreasonably withheld. My problem was solved, since I could turn right around and sub-lease that property to America's Tire.

The ink on the contract was barely dry when I asked the landlord for a sublease approval. She told me she would not agree to a sublease unless I told her how much money I was going to make on the property! This woman had been so nice to me when we negotiated the terms of the lease, but now she became a completely different person. She told me that she knew my company had only ten locations with annual sales in the millions, while America's Tire had hundreds of locations with sales in the billions, and she wanted to know how much I was going to be paid for the sub-lease. I told her my company was under no obligation to give her this information. I pointed out how the lease clearly gave us the right to sublease, and that consent would *not* be unreasonably withheld. When she would not budge, we threatened to sue her for breach of contract. She held out until the day before we were scheduled to go to court, and she agreed to approve the sublease only if I paid all her legal fees! I agreed, and on November 30, 1997, the very profitable deal with America's Tire went through.

About this time, I began negotiating with Tim for a buyout of his share in our partnership. For quite some time, he had been of only minimal help to me in the business, and our personal friendship had faded into little more than an old acquaintance. I have talked about this in an earlier chapter, how I complained to Reneé about my unhappiness with Tim as a business partner. She had advised that I talk with him about a buyout, but then Reneé got sick and I did not pursue the idea. By the late 1990s, I figured the time had come for us to talk about the partnership.

When I brought this up with Tim, he was open to the idea, and we agreed to start the process for a buyout. Boy, did that turn into a mess. I found out that a twenty-two-year business partnership is like a twenty-two-year marriage, and Tim treated the split more like a divorce than the end of a partnership. Finally, he sat down one day with my accountant and they went over the numbers. After some tradeoffs, Tim agreed to sign the papers for the buyout.

When I had first partnered with Timothy Bagdonoff in 1976, it seemed like a great idea. Looking back, although the partnership had some advantages, if I could do it all over, I would not have partnered with anyone in business. That is one of those lessons that you just learn along the way.

CHAPTER TWENTY-SIX
PROBLEMS WITH GOODYEAR

A couple years before I ended the partnership with Tim, my son Craig accepted an offer to come and work for me. Craig had graduated from high school with good grades, but he had no interest in going to college, so he took a job selling memberships at a fitness center. Since his walkie-talkie days, Craig had shown himself a natural at talking to people, and he did well in his sales job. But the hours were hard, and he was not making a lot of money. Shortly after starting with *Goodguys*, one of my warehouse managers said to me, "You need to put your son in the position of telemarketer." He told me some things about Craig which I already knew, that he could sell snow to an Eskimo and was not afraid to talk to anybody. So, I moved him to marketing, where he immediately began building a customer base and soon had three giant customers buying from him.

Craig

When the Firestone recall hit in 2000, and there was a sudden demand for billions of dollars' worth of tires to replace the ones that were recalled, Craig made a very wise decision. Rather than going after the retailers who could afford to buy only a dozen or so tires, he went for the new-car dealerships who had a national account billing. The dealers would issue a purchase order, and we would collect our money the next day in the form of a credit memo from Goodyear. My son brought a lot of business to our company, and he became my highest paid employee. By that time, he had a wife and three children, so it was a good situation for him.

Meanwhile, my youngest son Danny graduated from San Francisco State University with a degree in botany. Danny loved working outdoors, and he never showed an interest in coming to *Goodguys*, but with his botany degree he found a job in the landscaping business near Watsonville.

Around the year 2000, I bought some property in Clovis to build a new store. For twenty years our old location there had done very well, and after we sold it to America's Tire it continued to do well. So, it seemed the time was right for *Goodguys* to build a new store in Clovis.

One day I got a call from Mike Lindsey, a store manager who had worked for me in Sanger. Mike said, "Are you looking to buy some property in Clovis to build a store?" I said, "Yes, what do you have?" He told me that Tom Smith, whom I knew, was trying to sell a piece of property on Herndon Avenue. I called Tom and asked if he could show me the location, and he said there was not much to it except dirt. After looking at the lot, I bought it, thinking there would be minimal development fees, since the property was still zoned for agriculture. What I soon learned is that the residents of a big subdivision just to the north had been promised by city officials a park along Herndon Avenue. Next thing I knew, the whole city came out against us! We went to a city hall meeting to discuss all of this, and about 150 locals showed up, bringing complaints about concerns like noise, congestion, and the promise of a park. We lost in our effort at city hall, but we went back and re-applied. After that, we held a town-hall meeting and invited the whole neighborhood for coffee and donuts, hoping we could explain to them our operation and how we were not a threat to them. Again, a large number of locals showed up, but most of them would not eat our donuts, and one guy threatened to beat me up. Interestingly, the guy who threatened me is one of the few who ate our donuts and drank our coffee.

It took me almost three years to get the property re-zoned, and to finally get a shovel in the ground. I ended up paying more to the city for development fees than for the property itself, and the re-zone came with a lot of conditions. We were not allowed to do major engine-repair work, we could not allow cars to be parked overnight, and we could not exceed a certain noise level. Those were some of the conditions and costs, but we got the store built, and on April 1, 2003, we opened for business. From day one, the business there took off. For sixteen years, the Clovis store on Herndon has never had a loss.

1425 Herndon Ave, Clovis

During that time, Goodyear had a vacant store on Shaw and Willow. This was the store originally opened by Bob Hooper back in 1979, and which had led to that showdown between me and Goodyear over the three-mile rule. Hooper had long-since gone broke, and after that the store was leased by Winston Tire. But Winston also went broke, and because it had pledged all of its leases as collateral in lieu of a big line of credit with Goodyear, when it defaulted on its debt, Goodyear ended up with the Shaw and Willow store, along with about eighty others.

Goodyear was losing money from the vacancy on Shaw and Willow, but at that time I was not getting along with them, and they would not talk to me about taking over the vacancy. In 2002, Rich Gibbons was promoted, and John Presson became the new district manager. One day Presson came by for a visit, bringing along John Briceno, the rep who had squealed on me about the Dunlop tires at Fulton Mall back in 1984. Presson told me, very nicely, that Goodyear would like to mend our relationship. He asked what they could do to earn my trust, and for me to start buying their products again? While keeping my eyes on Presson, I pointed to Briceno and said, "Get me a new rep, because I don't trust this one." Briceno did not like that, so he turned around and walked out. Then I said to Presson, "It's obvious that Goodyear has been paying rent on a vacant store in Fresno and is doing all they can to put one of my competitors in that store. Are you guys having difficulty filling that location?" Presson did not give an answer, and he just went back to saying that we had a bad relationship, and was I interested in repairing it? I said I would try, but that I could not see myself working with John Briceno.

About two weeks later I got a new rep named Scott Thayer, who worked hard and really tried. One day Thayer asked if I wanted to take over several stores that Goodyear held the lease on. One was in Madera on Cleveland Avenue, one was in Visalia on Mooney Blvd., and the other was the Fresno store on Shaw and Willow. The stores in Madera and Visalia would actually have to be purchased from Heffner Tire, but Goodyear would need to approve my G110 contract for the deal. Initially there were some complications, but it all got worked out and Goodyear approved. I agreed to take over the three stores, but I was concerned about Shaw and Willow because I knew Goodyear had only eighteen months left on that lease. When I brought this concern to the Goodyear real estate department, I was assured they had two five-year options on the property, and those options would be exercised when the time came. That is what they told me, and I believed them.

    I took over the three stores in November of 2002. In the Shaw and Willow location, I put in more than $100,000 to get it up to par. We cleaned it, painted it, installed equipment, and changed all the display material. On November 13, 2002, we opened for business. With the 2003 addition of the new Clovis store, *Goodguys* now had eleven stores, plus the wholesale division.

    During the time that I was running Shaw and Willow, I started getting a lot of pressure from the city of Fresno over the warehouse on G Street. I had been doing business there since 1989, but in 2002 the city declared tires a high hazard, like storing oil or gasoline. They told me that because the location did not have the capacity for an Emergency Suppressant Fire Protection (ESFR) sprinkler system, which could put out over 300 gallons of water a minute, my warehouse was unsafe for storing tires. Also, the building could not be converted to handle an ESFR, and even if it had, the city did not have enough water available to feed such a system.

    I looked all over town and could not find an existing warehouse like what we needed, so I ended up buying some property to build my own at 2478 Golden State Blvd. I had some plans drawn up, and construction got started. Eighteen months later, I had a warehouse complex with two buildings, one with 50,000 square feet of space and with ceilings 24-feet high, and the other with 15,000 square feet of space, for a total capacity to store about 65,000 tires. When it was finished, I started moving all my inventory into it, and I also moved our corporate office there. Finally, everything was ready, and we opened the new warehouse on October 20, 2003.

2478 Golden State Blvd.

Shortly after we opened the Clovis store, we started construction on a 10-bay, 8,400 square foot store at 6760 N. Blackstone Avenue. We already had a store at 6670 N. Blackstone, but it was hidden behind a shopping center and I was subleasing the building from Goodyear. Steve Mele, the realtor I use, called me and said the property on the corner was for sale. I bought the property, drew up plans, and built an additional 4900 square foot office next door, where my accounting office is now.

The purchase of that property taught me the importance of LOCATION. We built that store and moved all the equipment from the old store approximately a hundred yards north. Because we were right on the corner, our visibility was perfect. I am not going to say we did not have any problems with that store. There are always problems with new construction. In the course of construction, we found out from PG&E that they did not have ample supply of electricity on the transformer across the driveway. We found this out two weeks before finishing construction. Our choice was to bore underneath Herndon Avenue and get power from Denny's restaurant across the highway.

Store at 6760 N. Blackstone

To make matters worse, AT&T informed us they did not have ample wire for telephone service for our building. They wanted us to trench across Long John Silver's drive-thru and Taco Bell restaurant. Can you see them allowing me to do that? AT&T had a six-inch conduit with one-half inch wire in it. If it were not for the owner of Ace Electric, whom I contracted with, I do not know what I would have done. Scott found the closest area to our building, opened it up and spliced into AT&T wire, and pulled telephone wire into our building as the AT&T employees watched.

We opened that store on April 1st, 2006. This was our flagship store, much larger than the old store, with more bays and a better location. The business immediately doubled from what we were doing at the old store, plus we owned the property rather than sub-leasing from Goodyear and not having to put up with their policy.

Meanwhile, at Shaw and Willow we were doing good business. I have mentioned how Goodyear assured me they would exercise their lease option, and how I had invested a lot of time, focus and money into getting that store up and running. But when the date came for the lease option to be exercised, without me knowing anything about it, Goodyear notified the landlord that they were not going to use the option, and they recommended the property be leased to one of my competitors, Discount Tire of Los Angeles (not to be confused with Discount Tire of Arizona). By the time I found out about this, the landlord had already negotiated a deal, and I had to move out.

This really threw a curve at me, and it put me on bad grounds with Goodyear for a long time. Since two can play the game, I quit buying from them, which is really the only thing that gets their attention. Actually, I was not trying to get their attention. I just did not want anything to do with them after the way they treated me, and after the loss I had to swallow on a store which *they* had asked me to take over from them. The people at Goodyear knew I was mad, and when their reps came by trying to mend the relationship, I would say, "Thanks, but no thanks." At that time, I really did not expect to ever buy another tire from Goodyear.

CHAPTER TWENTY-SEVEN
MARIO ANDRETTI COMES TO FRESNO

One day in 2005, Scott was in Bakersfield calling on a customer, and he ran into a Firestone representative named Jim McPoland, whom both of us knew. Scott said to him, "Hey, Jim, this might be a good time for you to call my dad." Next thing I knew, Jim called, and since he lived in Fresno, we arranged a meeting where he said he would like to see me sign on with Firestone. Not long after that meeting, Jim called to tell me he had spoken with his bosses, and that some of Firestone's higher echelon people had agreed to meet with me at a convention they were having at a dealer conference during the SEMA show in Vegas.

In October, I went to the convention in Vegas, and after meeting with some of the Firestone reps at the Bellagio Hotel, they agreed to talk with their superiors about signing me on as a Firestone dealer. A couple weeks later, one of their reps contacted me and asked what I would commit to doing for Firestone if they signed me on. I told him I would commit to purchasing a million-plus-dollars of product in the first year. That sounded good to the rep, and over the next few weeks we negotiated an agreement. They put out a very simple program for my company to get on board, so I went through the program and took all of my marketing discounts, advertising discounts, and regional discounts which they offered for the first year. I became a Bridgestone/Firestone dealer, and eventually they agreed to pay the costs for identification on my stores.

Later that year, B/F invited me to Cabo San Lucas in Mexico, where I met their President, John Gamauf. When I introduced John to Charlesia, as they shook hands, he stared at her ring and said something like, "I've never seen a diamond that big!" We started talking, and John told me he was looking for a diamond ring for his fiancée, Kimberly. I said, "I have a good friend in Fresno who is a diamond importer and a jewelry manufacturer. Next time you are in my area, why don't you stop by? I will introduce you to him, and I'm sure he'll have what you need." John said he planned to be in that part of California in February, and he asked if I could arrange a meeting. I told him I would do that.

When I got home, I called my good friend, Nader Malecon. Nader's family had fled from Iran when the Ayatollah took over in 1979, but they were able to leave with a lot of their wealth, including their diamonds. For years, Nader and I had an ongoing trade account, and when I asked him about a meeting with John Gamauf in February, he agreed. "It will be good timing," I told him, "because Firestone is planning to bring Mario Andretti to Fresno next year for a two-day appearance to promote Bridgestone/Firestone products." Since I was now a Bridgestone/Firestone tire dealer, Mario's coming to Fresno would be a boost for Goodguys as well as for B/F.

John Gamauf is a unique and interesting person who did a lot to help B/F after its 2000 recall of more than 14 million tires. Every tire they had ever put on a Ford Explorer between the years 1990 and 2000 had to come back, and even for a corporation as a large as Bridgestone/Firestone, that was a major threat. Not only did they have the cost of replacing all those tires, but the bad publicity had to be dealt with. That is when they promoted John, who is known for his personality skills, to president of the corporation. He is one of those rare people who knows no strangers and can talk with anyone. Basically, his whole job that year was to travel the country and promote Bridgestone/Firestone, and during that entire episode, they did not lose a single dealer. John did a great job, spending more than 300 days on the road, a lot of them with Mario Andretti, assuring dealers one-by-one that his company would come through this, and that if they stayed with B/F, they would be taken care of. I do not think it is an exaggeration to say that John Gamauf almost single-handedly saved his corporation in that difficult time, and this earned for him enormous respect in the industry. (Later, in 2011, John was inducted into the tire industry Hall of Fame.)

February came, and John flew into Fresno from his home in Nashville. Scott and I drove him, along with Jim McPoland, to Nader's office. We passed through the high security and were buzzed into a large room where Nader waited, surrounded by diamonds on display like one of my stores has tires on display. The room had no windows but was well lit, with two desks and some comfortable chairs set out for us.

When we were all seated, John showed Nader a list of careful instructions that Kimberly had written out for him. Nader looked at the list and said, "I think I've got what you want." He stood and walked to his safe, and a minute later he came back with a gorgeous, five-carat diamond, similar to Charlesia's. Nader held it out to John and said, "This diamond was mis-graded when I bought it, so it cost me a lot less than what it's really worth. If I took it to a professional grader, it would be re-graded and would cost hundreds of thousands. Since you are a friend of Pete's, I'll give you a discount."

You should have seen John, sitting in that chair and letting out a big sigh of relief! He quickly agreed to buy the diamond, and he and Nader worked out the arrangements. I had liked John from the day I met him, and it was nice to be able to help him get the right diamond for his fiancée. As we left, he thanked me for helping. I told him, "You're welcome, John." As we talked, I told him how I planned to set things up for when Mario Andretti came to town in June. I said, "When Mario comes, I hope you'll be here too." John said he hoped to be able to work that into his schedule.

When I got back to my office, I called my friend Daniel Bonyhadi and invited him out for lunch. When we got together, I told him about Mario coming to Fresno. I said, "Daniel, Mario Andretti is coming to town for two nights and one day, to promote Goodguys and Bridgestone/Firestone tires. Basically, what I have planned is for Mario to visit several of my stores and do autograph signing sessions, and to do some radio and television advertising to promote our new partnership with Bridgestone/Firestone."

Daniel's eyes had lit up as soon as I started talking. When I finished, he said, "Hey, would you be interested in working in a fundraiser for the Boys and Girls Club of Fresno?" I said, "Fine, but what will we do?" He said, "Let me handle it. You do your autograph signing sessions at your stores and all the stuff with radio and television, and I'll take it from there." We agreed that Daniel would organize the project, and I would do the advertising.

In June of 2006, Mario came to Fresno on a Wednesday night. Scott and I, along with John Gamauf and Jim McPoland, all had dinner with the legendary racer. We went to a nice Italian restaurant not far from my house, and as we sat at the table, people began recognizing who was there. Word started spreading through the restaurant, and next thing we knew, people were lining up for autographs. I was impressed with Mario's patience and generosity as he interrupted his dinner conversation again and again to sign autographs.

Daniel had planned for breakfast the next day at Fort Washington Country Club, and I invited all the city officials from Fresno and Clovis. In the morning, Charlesia and I rented a limo and picked up Mario and his publicist at their hotel. From there we drove to the Country Club, where all the city dignitaries, about fourteen of them, were waiting. Everyone had a great time, and the officials gave Mario the key to the city of Fresno.

After breakfast, we went to our newly opened store on Herndon Avenue in Clovis, where we had advertised open invitations for an autograph-signing session. In a four-hour period, we probably had more than a thousand people show up in a store that normally has about twenty customers a day. Mario stayed until he had signed every single autograph.

After we left the store, we went to the Elbow Room, one of the nicest pubs in town. Daniel had organized a private cocktail party where we had wine from Mario's personal winery, with tickets at $125 per person. Mario was there for about two hours, drinking his wine, talking to people, and signing autographs. After that, we went to the home of Daniel's friend, Jerry De Young, who has a banquet room that can hold a hundred people. Daniel had sold tickets for $500 a plate, and the room was full.

During the whole time of Mario's visit to Fresno, we netted $24,000 and donated it to The Boys and Girls Club. Bridgestone/Firestone's decision to bring Mario Andretti to Fresno did a lot of good for the city, for our business, and for the sale of Bridgestone/Firestone products. Also, it was great to meet and spend time with a racing legend, and to see what a down-to-earth and friendly person he is.

Mario Andretti in Fresno (c. 2006)

Charlesia, Mario and me (c. 2006)

Mario, Scott and Pete

Mario signing autographs

CHAPTER TWENTY-EIGHT
BACK IN LOVE WITH GOODYEAR

In May of 2007 I turned over the retail business to my son, Scott. I had been thinking about this for a while, and finally it seemed the time had come. What happened is that we had received a consumer complaint that went up to the Bureau of Automotive Repair, and I really did not want to deal with that stuff anymore. I drove with Scott and my attorney to the Bureau's office in Fresno, to discuss the complaint. After the meeting, when we got in the car I said, "Scott, I'm tired of the retail business. I have got an opportunity to sell it, or I can give it to you. Do you want it?" He said, "Dad, that's why I'm here." I said, "Good, you can have it."

News Review on Goodguys, 2007

I instructed my attorney to set up a corporation for Scott. We agreed to call it *Shubin Tire, Inc.* I funded that corporation for $30,000, and we split off the retail stores from the wholesale business. We notified our employees in retail that they no longer worked for *Goodguys Tire Center* but for *Shubin Tire, Inc.* Since then, Scott has run the retail business under my

Management Agreement Program, and he does a good job. I did keep the rights to be the administrator for his company, working with a small team of employees to provide administrative services for the eight retail locations.

From the time I hired Scott in 1990, he showed himself a natural for the job. Just like in his days as an All-American in team sports, he gets the respect of those on his business team. When he first came to work for me, I started him from the ground up. He was hard working and showed that he had what it took to eventually run the business. I wanted Scott, and all my sons, to have something better than what I had, working away my childhood for my father and then leaving home with twenty dollars. You could say I gave Scott the silver spoon to eat with, and he has done well. I am very proud of my son.

Although it was nice to have handed the business to Scott, it was like turning the car keys over to a sixteen-year-old who thinks he does not need anyone helping him know how to drive. We struggled for a while, with me trying to offer advice and him not wanting to hear. But I understand that he wanted to be left alone to run the business the way that seemed best to him. So, my business focus now consisted of running wholesale and providing administrative services for retail.

By this time, Craig had left our business for a move to Florida. I never wanted to see him leave, and I asked a friend of mine to try and talk him out of it. But Craig's marriage had failed, and his mind was made up to relocate and start something new. Although he had made a lot of money working for me, rather than saving and investing, he and his wife had spent it all. After moving to Florida, Craig had several different jobs, but he never succeeded financially like he did with *Goodguys*.

I miss having Craig around, but everyone must make their own decisions. Meanwhile, about a year after turning over retail to Scott, Goodyear appointed a new sales rep named Steve Uriyu. Steve was really a good rep who had been with Goodyear for many years. If he had been in that position when I got pushed out of Shaw and Willow, I am sure he would have put his foot down and not allowed it to happen. Goodyear also replaced John Presson with a new regional manager named Chet Warwick. Once a month, Chet and Steve would come by and try to talk with me about mending my relationship with Goodyear. The first time they came, I reminded them about what had been done to me at Shaw and Willow. Chet told me he was sorry this had happened, and he said he would not have allowed it if he had been in the position he now held. I believed him, and I believed that neither one of those guys would have allowed it, but I told him, "Chet, I'm sorry, but I made myself a promise that I would never buy another Goodyear tire." As they were leaving, I told them my door was open to them at any time, but that I would not be willing to buy from Goodyear ever again.

Chet did not give up. He came back to see me several times, and he was always very pleasant, showing a lot of patience and respect. One day on a visit he said, "Hey, Pete, maybe you can help me." He told me he had some product that was "stale dated," meaning it had been sitting in their warehouse more than ninety days, and under company policy they had to get rid of it. He told me the tires were discounted by an additional twenty percent below my normal wholesale buying price, along with all the behind-the-scenes discounts. He asked if I would consider buying two truckloads, which would be about twenty-four hundred tires.

I looked at the list of products, and I said, "Chet, you're really a nice guy, and you've been knocking at my door and you've been waiting for me to buy some tires. I had promised myself I would never buy another Goodyear tire, but you are really twisting my arm." I looked a little more at the list, and then I said, "How many tires are on this list?" He told me, "About eighty-two thousand." That would equate to about $8.2 million at regular wholesale price. I said, "Chet, you guys cost me a lot of money at the Shaw and Willow store." I kept my eyes on his while he nodded, and then I said, "I'll tell you what I'll do. I will buy all of the tires on this list, all eighty-two thousand, but I want fifty percent off the price *after* the twenty percent discount." What that meant was an offer to buy all those tires for about forty cents on the dollar. Chet looked at me with surprise, since he had only asked me to consider buying two truckloads. He said, "You mean you'll buy *all* of them?" I said, "Yes, I'll buy them all." He smiled and told me he would see about getting the deal approved through Akron.

Less than two hours after Chet left, he called to tell me that Akron had approved the deal. He said, "When do we start delivering?" Well, my warehouse was already full, so I had nowhere to stock 82,000 tires, but I told him to start right away. Within a week, the trucks started pulling up to our warehouse. Because of the huge discount, we were able to sell the tires at a markup before they even got delivered. We knew in advance when each shipment was coming, and how big it would be. Almost every day, shipments of up to 3,000 tires were coming in, and they were all going out the same day! I had purchased $8 million worth of tires for barely over $3 million, and in about sixty days they were all sold and delivered.

But there was a catch to this. In the retail tire business, there is an association of three groups of foreigners, each run by a godfather-type of leader. Together, these three groups control about a thousand tire stores in the western half of the United States. Goodyear had their reasons for not wanting me to sell to these groups, and they asked me nicely, several times, not to do it. I told them that if they do not want me selling tires to these guys, then why not cancel their associate contracts, and that way I could not sell them tires without forfeiting my backdoor bonuses? But Goodyear said they did not want to do this. That sounded fishy to me, and I was making a lot of money doing legitimate business with about 200 of the stores controlled by these groups, so I kept selling to them. In fact, I sold them most of the 82,000 tires.

This really caused a stir, because the retail market started getting flooded with very low-priced Goodyear products. The foreigners were using the cheaply priced tires to draw business to their stores, most of which were not fully equipped auto-repair centers, but rather were little more than store fronts with a few pieces of equipment like a tire changer, a wheel balancer and floor jacks. That is not how Goodyear wanted their tires sold, but they had allowed me to sign up more than two hundred of those foreigners as associate dealers of *Goodguys Tire* on a Goodyear wholesaling program.

The flood of cheap tires was very upsetting to a lot of independent dealers selling Goodyear products, and they started complaining. In other words, the hundreds of stores selling tires at below the normal retail price was hurting the market for other dealers. Well, word got out to Goodyear that I had sold those discounted tires to the groups who were now flooding the market with cheap products, but Goodyear never told this to the dealers who were complaining. They did not want their unhappy dealers to know they had sold those tires to me at an incredibly low price, so they told them a large amount of tires had been stolen from their warehouse yard, and the low-priced tires flooding the market were probably from that burglary. Goodyear went so far as to ask their unhappy dealers to help them get serial numbers on the tires, giving the appearance that they were trying to trace the tires back to who had originally sold them, when in fact they knew exactly where the tires had come from.

After I had sold the 82,000 tires, I learned a new way to make a quick profit by basically transferring tires at wholesale price to hundreds of the stores controlled by the three groups on Goodyear's bad-guy list. The way the wholesale program worked is that we would ask a tire-store manager to sign on as an associate Goodyear dealer. We would then submit an application to headquarters in Akron, and once Akron verified the existence and legitimacy of the store, Goodyear would assign them an account number as an associate of *Goodguys Tire*. This meant that we could sell them Goodyear tires at *whatever price we negotiated with them*, and Goodyear would give us a wholesaling discount of about ten percent.

Well, I had figured out that if I sold tires to those groups at my wholesale cost, along with the 10% wholesaling discount, Goodyear would issue me a 90-day billing, and if I paid far enough in advance of that 90-day deadline, I would make another two percent on what is called an anticipation discount. Along with this, there was also a two percent cash discount, along with a five percent advertising co-op. This meant that if I did things right, I would profit by a markup of 19%, just by selling tires to those dealers at the same price I was paying for them! I was getting all my profit on Goodyear's backdoor money. On each truckload of about a thousand tires purchased wholesale from Goodyear, I would send it for the same price to one of those dealers, and I would come away with a $15,000 profit. All of that, just for delivering a truckload of tires!

We kept this business going strong for several years, and how it ended is a story I will tell in the next chapter.

CHAPTER TWENTY-NINE
END OF THE ROAD WITH GOODYEAR

I continued selling tires to the hundreds of stores controlled by the three groups of foreigners. Those dealers were a big part of my business, but Goodyear continued asking me to stop selling them tires. I did not understand why Goodyear kept saying this, until one day I learned there was a lot more to the story.

It turns out that Goodyear had a big wholesaler in Los Angeles who had been making a huge profit by selling to those same foreigners, and I had taken away that wholesaler's business! The guy in L.A was doing, overall, about $50 million a year with Goodyear, whereas I was doing about $12 million. After a few years, the L.A. wholesaler gave an ultimatum to Goodyear. Either cancel me, or he would take his business elsewhere.

Goodyear had to make a choice, and the easiest thing for them was to not renew my contract and thereby keep their business with the guy from L.A. At the end of 2011, when my contract came up for review, Goodyear did not renew it. I found out when a certified letter came to my office. As I read it, I understood what it was saying, but I do not remember any of my thoughts. Suddenly I was cut out of more than ten million dollars a year in business which

I could not replace with another supplier. I walked over to Scott's desk and set the letter in front of him. I remember watching him read it, but I do not remember what he said. A huge cloud had come over my head, and I honestly cannot remember much else from that day. This was the worst of all times in my career as a businessman.

In 1964 I had left home with twenty dollars, and for almost fifty years I worked hard to build a business that provided for my family, for my employees, and for my community. What I had built meant a lot to me, and losing so much, so fast, hit me harder than I could ever explain to anyone else. I admit that I made some mistakes along the way, and I admit that at times I was arrogant. But I believed in what I was doing, and I made a lot of sacrifices to build what I had. Losing that much of my business overnight seemed to me like the end of the world, and I gradually went into a very deep depression.

Unless somebody has been through a depressed state of mind, it may be hard to understand the experience. Day after day I felt my mood sinking, like I was walking into a fog that kept getting thicker. I would try to tell myself, "Pete, you're okay. Come out of it! Come out of it!" But I could not come out of it. I began to care less and less about anything, and I did not want much to do with anybody. Charlesia was very supportive during that time, and so was Danny. Scott showed a lot of concern, but he was busy trying to keep the business going. As I became more and more withdrawn, and because of the silly things I was saying, even Scott began to pull away from me.

At Scott and Charlesia's urging, I went to see a psychiatrist. After talking with him, he prescribed a medication which I took for only a short time. In my case, the medication was not helpful, and after that, I began seeing a psychologist for weekly talk sessions.

Each Wednesday I would sit in a chair in the psychologist's office while he tried to talk me out of the depression. He would say things like, "Pete, there is no good reason for you to be depressed. You still have more money than you can spend. You have a family. You have a son who is running the retail business." Then he would basically tell me, "I really don't know what you are depressed about."

The psychologist had a point, because although I had suffered a major blow in business, I was far from broke and there was still a lot of business without Goodyear. But depression is not always a rational experience, and I could not grasp any of the sensible things the psychologist and others were trying to point out to me.

The depression lingered on, month after month. I came to a point where I only wanted to be alone in a room in my house, and I would not have cared if someone had taken all the money out of my bank account and stolen it. I would not have cared if someone had taken all my property and all my equipment. I was in a prison inside of my mind, and I could not relate to anything outside of that prison.

Charlesia became concerned that I was suicidal, because I started talking about some really silly things, making comments like, "If I die, I want to be buried next to Reneé." I agreed to be admitted into a private institution called the Community Behavioral Health Center, and I stayed there for a little more than a week. It was a lot like being in prison. They had gates, they had guards, and we could not leave. All around me, I saw other people having a good time playing basketball, taking art classes, and having open discussions when we all gathered for group therapy. But I could not break away from what was holding me in the depression. After about ten days, I called my wife and told her to come and pick me up. I checked out of the treatment center, and for a while after that I rarely left home and did not want to talk to anybody. Then, suddenly one day, I began snapping out of it.

In my business, we have a tradition of getting together on the day before Christmas to exchange gifts. Well, on Christmas-Eve of that year, I was sitting alone in my office, and from out past my door I could hear everyone having a great time. It started really sinking in that I am the founder and administrative head over this business, and I was not invited to the Christmas party! The more I thought about it, the more it made me mad. Right then and there, I started coming out of the depression. I gathered my stuff, then quietly left the office and went home to think things over.

Later that afternoon, I was still trying to shake what was left of the depression, but I knew the fog had lifted. I told Charlesia that I was over it, and I asked if she wanted to go out to dinner. She was happy to hear that, and off we went to our favorite Mexican restaurant, the Plaza Ventana. At the table, the more we talked and enjoyed our meal, the more I came out of what had held me in its grip for two years.

A few days after Christmas, I invited all the staff out for a luncheon, except for those working directly for Scott in retail. I reminded everyone that they do not work for Scott, but for me. Scott had kept things going while I was basically absent, but now I was back, and if anyone had a problem, they were to come to me and not to Scott. They all welcomed me back, and things returned to normal. That is the way it has been ever since.

CHAPTER THIRTY
MOVING ON

In 2011, a company called NTW, owned by TBC, had approached me about leasing my warehouse. In 2013, at Scott's urging, I called NTW's vice-president, Marty Krcelic, and asked if his company was still interested. He said they were, so I told him we were ready to negotiate a deal. At that time, I was still in my depression, so I asked Ted Starkel and Scott to do all the negotiations. They did a great job, and after NTW made a good offer on a long-term lease, I gave my approval. As part of the deal, NTW agreed to buy all the tires and equipment I currently had in the warehouse, meaning I would not need to move anything out. I only had to guarantee that I would make the payables against the inventory. They wrote me a big paycheck, and that provided a needed source of income after losing the business with Goodyear. We moved our accounting office to a building which Randy had remodeled next to my store on Blackstone and Herndon.

For the next couple years, there were no big developments in my business or personal life. We did not travel because of Charlesia's health, and there was not a lot for me to do at the office. I was able to focus on the kind of projects that I enjoy, like putting solar paneling on my house.

I learned from my CPA that I could get about half the cost of solar installations back on tax deductions in the first year. Also, with the depreciation, I could end up getting the solar very cheap, and after that I would have free electricity! That opened my eyes to how simple solar is, and to the opportunities for investment. I put $350,000 into solar for three of my commercial buildings, and I became the electricity provider for two of my locations plus my own office.

At that time, I was having breakfast often with my brother Alex, mostly talking about old times. One day I explained to him how simple the solar business is, and he seemed interested. Not long after that, I was having breakfast with Randy, the general contractor who built my house, and we got to talking about the solar business. I said, "You know, we've got my brother Alex, who is a professional salesman, and we've got you, a general contractor currently without a job, and we've got me, who can fund a new venture. Why don't we all agree to go into the solar business?" Randy lit up to the idea, and when I talked with brother Alex about it, he agreed to come and work with us if we started the company. After those commitments from Randy and Alex, I got busy with what needed to be done.

I had some extra space in my office, so I set up a place for us to run our solar business. We made Alex the head of sales, and Randy would do the installations. What I was really interested in was not so much to sell solar to residential customers, but rather to commercial businesses that wanted to reduce their electricity bill. I got busy making calls and negotiating deals where I would own the solar installation, and the business would get a fifteen percent discount on their electricity bill from the previous year, along with being protected from any raises in electricity prices for the duration of the contract.

Then I talked with my brother Bill and told him about the business I had started with brother Alex. Bill said he was really not so interested in a solar installation, but he wanted to make a big purchase as a way of trying to reconcile with brother Alex, who had rarely spoken with Bill for the past thirty years. Bill and I worked out a deal for him to purchase an installation for his house and for three commercial buildings, which meant about a half-million dollars in revenue for our solar company.

We got started with the installation on Bill's house, and one day I said to Alex, "Why don't you bring your crew over to brother Bill's house, so that Keith, our electrician, can go over with you guys how a solar system works." Alex told me he did not want to be a part of anything involving Bill, and that if he wanted to learn something about how a solar system works, he would "go to school for it." That was real disappointing for me and for Bill, and after doing the installation on the house, I backed out of the rest of the deal.

Alex and I had been working together well for about nine months, but after that situation, tension developed between us. Eventually, Alex ended up resigning. With my brother out of the business, a couple of the salesmen from his crew approached me about taking over his position as head of sales, but I did not feel comfortable with any of them. In the early part of 2018, I decided to close the business, although I continue to invest in solar here and there.

I do not buy tires anymore, and I do not have the same energy for business, but I am always looking for an opportunity to build a new store. I have become more of a landlord in recent years, investing heavily in property, and I get a royalty of about three percent from each location run by one of my franchisees (except for the five run by Scott, whom I do not charge a royalty).

In my office, I have six employees who handle important administrative work for nine store managers. At the end of each day, the managers gather their paperwork and go through a checkout sheet to show that everything is balanced. Then they put it all in a bag for a driver to pick up the next morning and bring to my office, where my staff goes through it. My staff verify the deposits at each store, file all of their invoices (which our computer system automatically tracks on every car that each store has worked on for the past four years, as required by law), and check all the numbers to confirm that we've had no pilferages, cash shortages, or other inconsistencies.

I keep an eye on the business of all my franchisees, the sales and profit numbers, the inventory and so forth. I go to my office at about ten, and by eleven I am looking to have lunch with somebody. By one I am back in the office, and at three I go home.

Two of my sons live in California. Danny, the youngest, currently does ground maintenance at Cal Poly University in San Luis Obispo. He likes his 8-hour workday and his time off, and the job Danny has fits him perfectly. He loves his wife, Maryann, and his son, Talon, more than any one I have seen.

As for Scott, he has five stores under his responsibility, and he is doing a great job of running them. He has a general manager who oversees all the daily responsibilities of the store managers, so basically Scott can just read the reports, then give his approval or instructions. He sets up the budgets for all the managers, and he communicates with his GM on a daily basis as to the strengths and weaknesses of the company. He continues to make a great salary to support his family, and I am very happy with how he has made good on his opportunities. Scott has three children, and one of his daughters, my granddaughter Claire, is in college at Dominion University in Northern California on a golf scholarship.

After all the struggles that Scott and I have gone through in how the business should be run, just recently he honored me publicly in a way that brought tears to my eyes. He did not tell me he was doing this, but one day as I walked out the door of my office, he said, "Hey, Dad, you want to see what we're doing in the stores?" Well, I knew he had redone the interior sales floors at each of his locations, but I had already seen that. I said, "What are you doing?", and he said, "Come on in here and look."

I followed him into the sales room of the store, and there, up on the wall, I saw a large, framed picture of myself. I had to look at it for a couple of seconds, to let it sink in. On the upper right corner, under a quote on my business ethics, are the words, *Pete Shubin, Founder*.

Founder plaque

Scott told me he had placed one of these in each of the stores. By doing that, he showed the respect and appreciation he feels toward me. I could hardly express in words how much it means to me, for my son to do that.

My other son, Craig, still lives in Florida, and his time of working for *Goodguys* remains the financial highlight of his life.

I urge him, with fatherly love and the wisdom of years, to focus on what he wants to accomplish, and on how his actions affect others. Having said that, I am proud of all my sons, and I know their mother would be proud of them also.

I do not golf anymore, only because my feet hurt from diabetic neuropathy, and I do not travel. I am still a Fox News diehard, a 49er and a Fresno State fan, a supporter of President Trump, and a busy grandfather. I am happy with my life, and I want to help Donald Trump make America great again.

Scott and his daughter, Claire

Danny and Talon

My granddaughter, Kailyn

My grandson, Jacob

Scott and his wife, Andrea

Me and Talon

Danny, Maryann and Talon

**Charlesia and me
at the family reunion**

Scott, speaking at the family reunion

CHAPTER THIRTY-ONE
SHUBIN FAMILY REUNION

Shubin family Reunion

The first Shubin Family Reunion

In semi-retirement, I still had job responsibilities but no longer a crushing daily workload. After all I had been through, and now passing the seventy-year mark, I started thinking a lot about my siblings. Since our father passed in 1987, most of my brothers and sisters had rarely spoken, and the only exceptions were Bill, Annie and me. After thinking about this for a while, one day in the summer of 2016 I saw a post on Facebook by one of my nieces, showing a nearly forty-year-old picture of my four brothers and me. In the post, my niece said something like, "Does anyone have a more current picture with all of them together?" Well, my son Scott posted a remark, saying, "You couldn't get those five stubborn old men in a room together for a picture even if you wanted to!" When I saw that, I took it as a challenge, and I decided the time had come to do something that might bring my family closer together.

The five Shubin brothers (c. 1972)

The five Shubin brothers (c. 2016)

Most of us Shubins barely knew each other, and some had never met at all, mainly because of the elders not getting along for so many years. So, I called each of my siblings and made the point that our parents would be ashamed of us if they were here to see us acting this way toward each other. I invited them all to our home for coffee and pastries, and to discuss the first ever *Shubin Family Reunion*! Everyone was on board, and we set a meeting date for September.

The day came, and with the exception of Annie in Australia, everyone showed up for our first time of being together since the 1980s. In my house we have a big, formal dining room, and we had chairs and sofas spread out so everyone could find a comfortable place. Bill and Martha came first, and then, one by one, the rest all showed up with their spouses.

Mike and Annie Slivkoff. Mike was a really nice guy. Sadly, he passed a couple months before the reunion.

The mood was a little stiff, but the meeting went well, and everyone agreed on a family reunion involving only immediate family members. Someone said, "Pete, if anyone could pull this off, it would be you." They agreed to let me handle the planning and preparations, and I made clear that I was not going to make this a religious event. We would plan to have an elder lead in a prayer at each meal, but there would be no services or requirements involving religious observances. I also said the reunion would be only for blood relatives and their families. No friends, boyfriends, girlfriends, or anything like that. The only thing I asked for help with was names, addresses and phone numbers for all the children. After spending a lot of time looking at our calendars, to see when everyone could get away for a few days, we decided on the weekend of May 5-7, 2017.

After the meeting I was excited and gung-ho about all of this, but I soon realized I did not know what I was getting myself into! I reserved thirty rooms, for three days and two nights, at a beautiful resort called Wonder Valley Ranch, about thirty miles from Fresno in the Sierra foothills near Sequoia National Park.

I had to decide how I was going to entertain a group of more than a hundred family members. The ranch has an indoor stage with seating for several hundred, so I liked the idea of having speakers for Friday and Saturday nights. After some shopping around, I hired a comedian named Reuben Quintana. Reuben was known for bringing off-color jokes and for a routine that was geared to a Hispanic audience, but he assured me he would avoid unsuitable language and would design his act appropriately for his audience. The plan was set for Friday night, but I still had to get something for Saturday. I called brother Alex and asked if he would be willing to speak. More than anyone else, Alex has a lot of knowledge of our family's history, and I believed a good speech from him on the importance of family would set a strong example and would do a lot to bring healing. Brother Alex agreed.

In the months leading up to the reunion, I sent out personalized invitations encouraging everyone to set aside the dates for attending what I advertised as *The First Shubin Family Reunion*. Each month I mailed everyone a newsletter, reminding them of the plans and giving updates on the activities that would be available. I also asked several family members to write something about the importance of a family reunion, and four of them did, including my beautiful wife. What Charlesia wrote really stirred my heart, and I printed it in one of the invitational newsletters. She said,

> *Greetings to all of you!*
>
> *For those of you who do not know me, I am Peter Michael Shubin's wife, Charlesia Ann Thomas Shubin.*
>
> *Peter and I met in 1993 and were married in 1994, thus creating a new family of two daughters, three sons and two large dogs named Tabetha and Barney.*
>
> *I am going to talk about families. I was adopted at birth, never knowing anything about my birth parents. This information came to me later in life. My father told me when I was five that I was adopted. He explained to me*

that he and my mother were not able to have a baby of their own. He stated that the doctor took them into a room filled with little newborn babies and he asked them to choose the one they wanted. They were so excited, telling me they chose the prettiest baby girl there. That was me. I was bundled up and they took me home with them. They raised me as their very own.

I always wondered where I came from. Was I born in Fresno? Did I have brothers and sisters? When I was sixteen and could date, might he be my brother? As much as I wanted to know my heritage, I would not investigate because I never wanted to hurt my sweet parents.

One summer when my mother's sister came to Fresno for a visit from Springfield, MO, she called me into a bedroom and closed the door. She wanted to visit with me. At this time, I was around thirty-five years of age. She asked me to sit down on the bed and told me that she wanted to talk to me. We visited for a while and she asked me if I was ever curious about my heritage. I told her I was but that I didn't want to hurt my mother and father. She proceeded to share with me a few things she knew. I was born at the Fresno County Hospital. My birth father was Italian and my birth mother was German. My birth mother was married. She and her husband had separated. She then became involved with another man – my birth father. She and her husband decided to reconcile. He informed her that he would not accept another man's child.

I was therefore, and thankfully, given up for adoption! I thank God every day in my prayers that I was. I could very easily have been aborted! But that was not God's plan for me. He gave me to the two most wonderful Christian people on earth. Who knows what would have happened to me if it were not for His plan.

I grew up as an only child. My parents were wonderful examples. We went to church every Sunday morning, Sunday night, Tuesday night and Thursday night. They were the kindest, sweetest and most thoughtful parents anyone could have asked for. They led by being Christian examples.

So, to all of you reading this, if you have brothers and sisters, TREASURE them. Do not waste time here on earth fighting and having ill feelings toward one another by being bad examples to your children. Life is too short! Our life in Heaven will be based on how we have lived our lives here on earth, how we treated our families and all loved ones! Life is too short! Learn to love and appreciate each other here on earth! After you die it will be too late to mend your brotherly and sisterly relationships. Your parents would be deeply unhappy and hurt by your negative attitudes toward each other. Spend the rest of your days here sharing your love one with another. Remember, you should be a godly example to your children, grandchildren, great-grandchildren and all the generations to come. You do not want your family's history to be filled with hate, but with love!

With the example of love shown to us in the Bible, and all the time, effort and energy that was put into the planning of this reunion, I sincerely pray that all of you will enjoy yourselves and spend time getting to know each other better.

Love one another as you would want to be loved!

With love to all, Charlesia Ann Thomas Shubin
Wife, Daughter, Mother, Step-mother, Mother-in-law, Grandmother, and Great-Grandmother

Everything seemed in place, but about two weeks before the reunion, brother Alex indicated he might not come. That put me on the spot. I called my friend, Lee Brand, who had recently been elected mayor of Fresno, and told him I needed a speaker to talk on the importance of family. Lee said he would have loved to be the speaker, but with his new position as mayor he could not commit to it. After talking with Lee, I called my friend, Nathan Magsig, a county supervisor whom I had known about twenty years and whose district included the Wonder Valley area. I had a good talk with Nathan, and he agreed to provide a speech that would emphasize the value of family.

The big day came. May the fifth. Families started arriving, some from as far away as Australia and Moscow, and others from Oregon, Wisconsin, Southern California and the Central Valley. Out of the 129 invited, only twenty-one did not show. We had 108 Shubins, all gathered on twenty-acres of lush landscape with oak and sycamore groves, scenic trails, wide open spaces and a clear-water lake, all in the shadow of rolling foothills leading toward the Sierra Mountains.

The first thing people noticed when arriving was the fresh smell of a breeze coming in off the nearby hills. The cottages were spread out neatly along tree-lined roads, and in every direction the landscape was an amazing blend of shapes and colors. Most of Friday was spent just getting everyone registered and situated in their lodgings. My grandkids, Kailyn, Claire, Madison and Jacob, did a great job facilitating all of this, and Jacob looked like a professional bellman helping people with their luggage.

At first there was a lot of confusion, but it was all coming together. The kids quickly got to know each other, and before I knew anything about it, some of them had agreed to swap rooms! I was okay with that, if they were all happy and getting along.

When everyone finally got settled in, it was time for dinner. Imagine more than a hundred Shubins seated at tables in a giant dining room with foods like barbeque steak, chicken, prime rib, salads and desserts. Wonder Valley really provided first class meals, and there was no shortage of food. Brother Bill said a blessing over the meal, while everyone else stayed silent in respect. Then the eating started. I enjoyed the food, but most of all I kept looking around in amazement.

After the meal, Scott introduced Ruben, and everyone settled in for a time of good entertainment. Ruben did not disappoint. He was funny, and his jokes were appropriate for the audience. His comedy routine was scheduled to last an hour, but everyone enjoyed it so much that he went on for two hours. Afterwards, he stayed for a while, mingling among the Shubins. It was just an incredible night, and I felt very satisfied.

Scenes from Wonder Valley Ranch

The next morning, everyone came out after breakfast to be a part of the events and activities that went on until dinnertime. Whenever I looked around, I saw family members talking with each other and enjoying the outdoor activities like horseback riding, tennis, basketball, softball, volleyball, horseshoes, boating and fishing at the lake, swimming in the pools, riding down water slides and bouncing on trampolines. The ranch also had a barnyard petting farm and beautiful trails for hiking and bicycling. It was a tremendous day for everyone. Charlesia and I were busy as host and hostess, but now and then I would stop to just look around, and what impressed me the most was how all the kids got along and enjoyed themselves, even though most of them were meeting for the first time.

At dinner, my brother-in-law, Alex, said Grace. Then, when we had finished with another great meal, Scott introduced Nathan. After opening with a prayer for our gathering, Nathan spoke on family values and the importance of family. At one point he said something like, "Without family, you have nothing." I really appreciated Nathan's talk, and as I looked around, I saw that everyone was paying attention. After the speech, Nathan stayed a while and mingled with the families, while his own kids mixed with ours for a summer evening with all that was available.

The reunion filled a void in my life. The feeling all through the weekend was very positive, and I felt so satisfied when brother Bill came to me at the end and said, "Pete, this was really a great reunion." My brother Jim told me the same thing, and so did Annie. As we started driving home, Charlesia said to me, "I'm glad you got your fulfillment out of that." My wife was very supportive of the whole thing, and she was right there with me for every step.

I had wanted to bring the members of my large family closer together, for the cousins to get to know one another, for broken relationships to start mending, and for me to get to know the nieces and nephews I had rarely seen for all their lives. Honestly, I did not see any mending of relationships among my brothers, but it was a great time for the younger family members who showed no interest in following the bad example of the elders.

CHAPTER THIRTY-TWO
A BIG SURPRISE FOR CHARLESIA

In an earlier chapter I mentioned how Charlesia was adopted at birth by Tommy and Charolene Thomas, the most wonderful man and woman she could possibly have been raised by. According to the story, the birth mother separated from her husband and became pregnant by another man. Later, when they wanted to reconcile, the husband did not want another man's child in the home, so the mother put her up baby for adoption. This is the story Charlesia had believed for most of her life.

After we married, each year on her birthday my wife would say something like, "I wonder if my birth mother is thinking of me?" When she would say this, I knew from the emotion in her voice that it was a big deal inside of her. She loved and appreciated her adoptive parents, but she yearned to know something about her origins.

After a few years of seeing this ache and hunger in my beautiful wife, I decided to do some research and see what I could come up with. This was about the year 2000, when the technologies for researching family history were growing. After some looking around, I spoke to a man in San Francisco who had access to the records of closed and sealed adoptions in California. He said he would do some research and get back to us. A short time later, the man called Charlesia with news that he had located her birth certificate and had also done further research. He said the certificate did not show a father, but it did provide the birth mother's name of Margaret Helmuth Santos. That was a big breakthrough, but we still needed a phone number.

I spoke to my credit manager who worked for me, and who could skip trace anybody through the credit bureau and get information on them. He got to work and came up with the birth mother's phone number! I gave all that information to Charlesia, and she was excited, but also scared to death to make the call. I think that for anyone who has not been through such an experience, of being adopted out at birth and always living with the mystery of her origins, it might be hard to understand the strong and conflicting emotions my wife was feeling. It took her six months to get up the nerve to call.

One day she decided to do it. She tapped in the number, and after a few rings a woman answered. Charlesia pulled in a deep breath and introduced herself. Then she said, "I understand that you are my birth mother." The woman was silent a moment, and then she said, "I gave you up for adoption, so I don't understand why you are calling me."

Charlesia felt those words like a punch in the stomach. After taking a few moments to regather her thoughts, she said, "I would like to know what nationality you are, and what nationality my birth father is." The woman answered sharply, "That's none of your business." Charlesia persisted, asking another question, saying, "I would just like to know if there are any illnesses in my background, or any medical information that I should know about?" Again, the woman told her, "It's none of your business." When Charlesia started to speak again, the woman cut her off and said, "Don't ever call me again." With those words, the mother hung up on her birth daughter.

I really have no words to describe what my wife was going through during and after that call. She did not say much about it, except that she never wanted to go through that again. After being stabbed once through the heart, why should she want to risk it again? As the years passed, on her birthdays she no longer thought about her birth parents, but she did continue to think and wonder about her siblings. Having been told that she was conceived through an affair, Charlesia assumed that if she did have siblings, they would not be full-blooded, but she still had a deep hunger to learn what she could about her original family.

My wife was eager for anything that could lead to a breakthrough, so when I spoke with her about sending her DNA information to Ancestry.com, she went through the process. After sending in the information, hoping it would lead to finding somebody matching her DNA, she waited and waited, but nothing came back.

In October of 2004, we went to the Fresno Fair and spotted a table with two women showing their company's know-how for doing genealogical research. We stopped, and Charlesia began talking with the ladies. After a while, I was wanting to leave but I could barely pull my wife away. When we got home, I decided to try again at doing some research. I went to the archives of the Fresno Bee Obituaries, and after some searching, I saw that Margaret Helmuth Santos had died in the previous year. The obit said, in part:

> *Margaret Helmuth Santos passed away on June 30, 2003, at the age of 81. She was preceded in death by her husband,*

Frank Santos. Margaret Santos is survived by Joan Madrizal, Carol Jorn, Frank Santos, Jr., and Spouts.

When I saw that Margaret's children were listed, I called 411 for information on those three names, but the only one whose number I could get was Joan's. That same day, with Charlesia sitting next to me, I called. Joan answered, and after introducing myself, I spent a little time helping her feel assured that this was not a prank phone call. When it seemed that Joan was ready to take me seriously, I asked if Margaret Santos was her birth mother. She said that she was. I then asked if this was the Margaret Santos who passed away on June 30, 2003, and again she said yes. Then I dropped the bomb, first telling her that my wife, Charlesia, had been adopted out at birth, and then saying that based on some recent genealogy work, "I believe you don't know that you have an additional sibling in your life. I believe that my wife might be your half-sister." Joan immediately said, "That can't be. No way. Absolutely not." I gave her a few seconds, and then I said, "Well, my wife is sitting right here, would you like to talk with her?" Joan agreed, and I handed the phone to Charlesia.

They talked for about ten minutes, with Joan taking notes as Charlesia gave information like the date and year of her birth and when she was adopted out. Then, after exchanging numbers, they hung up. During and after the call, Charlesia felt so overwhelmed that to this day she barely remembers what she and Joan talked about.

We later learned that after the call, Joan called her sister Carol and told her, "We have a sister we never knew anything about," but neither of them told their brother Frank! Maybe it was just too much for them to try and process. I do not know. All I do know is that Joan never called back. A week passed, and then a year.

Joan had been very kind on the phone, and as the years rolled by without us hearing anything, my wife assumed that with so much of life having already passed for all of them, maybe Joan just did not want to deal with this. Charlesia had prepared herself for this possibility, and she did not become bitter. Yet the whole situation was so hurtful and disturbing, especially the coldness of the birth mother's rejection, that she did not want to talk much about it at all. The matter rarely came up, and life went on.

One day in December of 2018, Charlesia got a surprising call. Actually, she had missed the call, but her phone showed it had come from a man named Frank Santos, Jr.! As close as I am to my wife, I can only imagine how this was for her, to be suddenly contacted by a man she assumed was her half-brother. It was beyond words, and the only thing Charlesia really said to me was, "It is such a bizarre thing. It has to have been from God."

She called Frank, and they talked for a long time. He said that he had done a lot of research in his genealogy, tracing it all the way back to the sixteenth century. After giving her more details to show how seriously he had researched his DNA, he told her the results showed he and Charlesia to be siblings. Of course, my wife assumed he meant *half*-siblings, but he told her, "No, we are full-blooded brother and sister."

Charlesia needed a few seconds for this to sink in. What Frank had just told her turned upside down the story she had believed for most of her life. During that phone call, she also learned that Joan and Carol are her full-blooded sisters, with Charlesia being the third oldest of the four. The information came at her like one giant wave after another, and all of this raised the question of *why* the third child of four had been adopted out? A lot can be speculated, but it seems the truth will stay hidden in a mystery forever.

After that first call, Frank and Charlesia talked frequently, sometimes daily. One day I asked her, "How does it feel to have a brother?" She laughed and said, "I really don't know how to act!" She was learning a lot from Frank, such as the fact that their ancestors were among the Spaniards who settled California in the 18th century. This was absolutely fascinating for Charlesia. Another twist came when they realized they lived only five miles from each other, and that Frank's favorite restaurant was the Plaza Ventana, the same place where I had been having lunch at least twice a week for years, sometimes with Charlesia! There is no telling how many times we all passed each other without having a clue. Frank also told her that Joan and Carol live just a few miles away, meaning that all of them had been living for many years within a five-mile radius.

The time came for a face-to-face meeting. Frank arranged a luncheon at the Plaza Ventana a couple days after Christmas. All four of them showed up, and the next thing Charlesia knew, she was at a table with her two sisters and her brother. She sat there, all of them looking at her, and she looking back at them, knowing they had come from the same father and mother, and yet they were complete strangers.

The luncheon lasted four hours, and afterward Charlesia could only say, "This is all very strange." When she told me the mood at their table was awkward, I said, "Why don't you invite them to our house?" I told her that for an occasion like this, with siblings meeting each other after seventy years (actually, Charlesia was 69, and Frank a couple years younger), it might be better to have a nice luncheon in a private home. She agreed, and when she called and offered the invitations, they all accepted.

The day came, and everyone arrived about two in the afternoon. Frank and Joan came with their spouses, and that is when I learned that Carol is widowed. I saw at first glance the strong resemblance between Charlesia, Joan and Carol. We all had a really nice time, with everyone feeling more relaxed, and all of us getting to know each other. Charlesia had told them it would be a luncheon, but we catered in enough food for two meals, so everyone stayed until eight.

My wife's birthday is March 22, and as I have said, for the twenty-five years we have been together, every year on her birthday she would go into deep reflections about the mystery of her original family. Well, on Charlesia's next birthday, for the first time in her life she received a card from a sister. It came from Joan, a card specifically designed for a sister. I wish I had the words to express my feelings as I watched my beautiful wife holding and cherishing that birthday card. You had to have been there. I do not know any other way to say it.

When we have family members whom we know for all our lives, we can take this for granted. But my wife was denied that experience. Her adoptive parents gave her a wonderful upbringing in a warm and loving home, and she is grateful for that. But now she has something new, with Frank, Joan and Carol. In her words, she feels that "a void has been filled." She told me, "Every time we talk, we have seventy years to make up for." After missing out on the memories of a lifetime together, the four siblings are moving forward in their relationships, wanting to learn all they can about each other's history.

Heather, Charlesia, Frank, Wendy, Carol and Joan

The first meeting!

CHAPTER THIRTY-THREE
THE SILVER ANNIVERSARY

In 2018, after Charlesia and I had privately celebrated our twenty-four-year anniversary, I started thinking about the twenty-fifth, the silver. One day I said to her, "Charly, next year let's have a twenty-five-year anniversary party!" She tightened her lips and said, "No way." I respect my wife's feelings, but I did not feel okay with skipping the celebration. She and I had married privately, with just the two of us at that little chapel in Pacific Grove, so I wanted to do something that our family members and friends could be a part of. Most of all, I wanted to honor Charlesia, who is the best wife any man could ever have.

I spoke about this with my daughter-in-law, Andrea, who is very skilled at putting functions together. I did not have to ask her twice. She was all for the idea, and when I said, "Andrea, I want a *first-class* anniversary party for Charly," she assured me that it would be first class. Not long after that, we got together to carefully go over the guest list. When we had decided on 52 invitations, she said to me, "What is the budget?" I told her, "We'll use my Gold Card," and I left it at that.

In the months leading up to the anniversary, as Andrea was planning and preparing all of this, I could not discuss it with her from home, so I did it from my office. I could see she was doing a great job. She reserved a back room at Fleming's Restaurant, created a great invitation card, put in an order for a cake, and managed to get everyone to not slip up and let Charlesia know about this. As the time got close, I made arrangements for Charlesia's daughters and son-in-law to fly in from Oregon. On Sunday, the day before the party, I told her that Scott and Andrea were taking us out to Fleming's Restaurant on Monday night for our anniversary. Everything was in place, and even though more than fifty people had known for months, my wife did not have a clue.

    Fleming's is a big restaurant, and the party room is way in the back. Charlesia and I had reserved the room before, so she knew the layout of the place. At about six o'clock on Monday night, as we entered Fleming's and started walking toward the back, she began wondering why we were not taking a seat at one of the empty tables. She was also looking around and wondering why there was no sign of Scott and Andrea. As we passed the last table in the row that ends near the door of the party room, all of a sudden, she froze. She turned toward me, and with a not-so-happy look on her face, she reminded me of a joke we have about an old sheep dog I owned. The dog would follow us anywhere, but if we opened the door to the truck, she knew the only reason for us putting her in the truck was to take her for a trim, so she would freeze up and refuse to go any further. Well, as my wife and I got near the door of that party room, she froze and said to me, very firmly, "I am *not* going in there." She was fit to be tied about me doing this, so I said, "Why don't you want to go in there? Do you think Andrea is going to bite you?" With that look still on her beautiful face, she turned back toward the door and we walked into the room.

    As we entered, we saw about fifty people suddenly stand and start clapping. When Charlesia saw everyone, she put on a happy face and did a great job of acting surprised. I was the only person in the room who knew she was fuming inside! She gave me a big hug in front of everyone, and she said in my ear, "Why did you do this?" I told her, "Because I wanted to."

She started making her way around, greeting everyone and thanking them for being there. I could see she was starting to really enjoy the night, but the biggest surprise of all was still coming. What she did not know is that Wendy and Heather would soon be walking through the door. They had planned to be there hours before the party started, but their plane got delayed and they landed at the airport right about the time their mom and I walked into the restaurant.

A little after 6:30, as Charlesia was talking with some guests, she looked up and saw her kids and son-in-law walking toward her. My wife does not get to see her children often, and any steam she was still holding in, it all came out. All was forgiven. She started hugging her daughters like she had not seen them in a hundred years, and as I watched her crying, it made *me* start to cry.

At about seven o'clock, the time came for me to make a toast to my wife. Because I do not like speaking in front of crowds, I was nervous and wanted to make it short and simple. As I lifted my glass to lead everyone in the toast, I looked at Charlesia and said, "To my best friend and my wife of twenty-five years. I am hoping for twenty-five more." I felt good as I saw how pleased my wife was with this, and with the whole night. She gave me a kiss and said, "You are my best friend, too."

Of the fifty-two people we invited, the only one who did not show up was Daniel Bonyhadi's widow, Lorna, who could not make it for health reasons. Everybody had an opportunity to speak, some whom I have known for fifty or sixty years. One of the people who spoke was Don Anderson, my oldest friend. Don and I grew up together from grade school, and we were notorious for getting into mischief. Even after we both got married, we still got into a lot of trouble together. He was one of those friends who, when he would come over, my wife would say "Good night", and then hope that she sees me in the morning. When Don had his turn to speak, he said I was one of his oldest friends, and he laughingly talked about some of the trouble we had gotten into without ever going to jail. Another highlight was when three of my grandkids stood up and said, "We have known this man all of our lives, and he is the best granddad anyone could ever have."

We really had a great time, and after everybody had their opportunity to talk, we got up and cut the cake. As I looked around the room, and as I saw how happy my wife was, I felt very fulfilled in my heart.

The party ended about ten, and I walked out with my arms around Charlesia and Andrea. We came to the front and stopped so that Andrea could sign for the bill with my Gold Card. When she looked at the size of the bill, she turned to me and said, "I didn't realize how much we drank!" I just smiled and said, "Andrea, you did a great job, and I appreciate it very much." Then I told her, "I really don't even want to see that bill." I never did look to see how much it all cost. All that mattered was that my wife had been honored, and that she was satisfied.

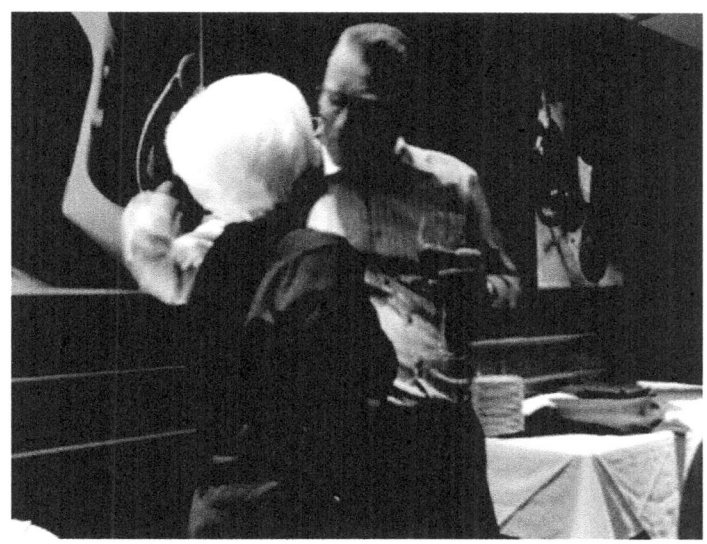

The Silver Anniversary!

At the anniversary celebration with Charlesia's daughters and son-in-law

CHAPTER THIRTY-FOUR
A LONG WAY FROM RAHMATABAD!

In chapter thirty I mentioned that "I do not buy tires anymore, and I do not have the same energy for business, but I am always looking for an opportunity to build a new store."

Well, since I wrote those words in chapter thirty, a full year has passed. That is how it can go when a busy 75-year-old is trying to find time to write his life story! During this past year, a lot has happened, but what I want to finish my story with is a brief account of the completion and opening of a $2,500,000 store run by Armen Petrosyan under my Management Agreement Program.

My purchase of the land for this store, in a newly developing shopping center by the corner of Herndon and Brawley, came about unexpectedly. For several years I had been wanting to build a store in that general area, and in 2015 I put into escrow a piece of property at Herndon and Blythe, having been assured by the realtor that he could get the property re-zoned for a commercial building. I was in no hurry, but after more than three years had passed, I was getting unhappy with the lack of progress. Well, one day in November of 2018 I received a surprise call from a different realtor. After introducing himself, he said something like, "I understand you've been trying to get a property re-zoned at Blythe and Herndon, and that you're having problems." I acknowledged that this was in fact the case, and then he told me, "Well, I have a parcel on Brawley and Herndon, less than a mile away from that property you've been sitting on." I was all ears as he went on to tell me the parcel down the road had already been re-zoned for a commercial building, and that it was basically ready to go to the city for a plan check. "It's ready to go," he said. "You get the plans drawn, and get your store built." I did not have to hesitate before telling him I was interested in looking at the parcel.

On the same day I drove to that corner and looked around. It appealed to me as soon as I saw it, right there in a developing shopping center with a couple of nice-looking stores and plans for others to be built in the near future. I told the realtor I wanted it, and he replied that he wanted twenty dollars a square foot, at forty-one thousand square feet. I said, "The other parcel I had in escrow was fifteen-dollars a square foot, so what makes this parcel worth twenty dollars?" He said "Make me an offer, and we'll see what we can do." We wrote the offer at fifteen dollars a square foot, and he quickly accepted.

A couple days later I told the other realtor, who had been working for years on getting a re-zoning permit for the property on Blythe, that I was thinking of backing out of the deal. He nearly broke into tears because this meant he would lose the commission he had worked so hard to get. Well, after giving it some more thought, I ended up closing escrow on that property also, after it was cleared for city zoning approvals. My purpose for that lot was not to run a store, but maybe to build one for a competitor and be a landlord. Today, the property is for sale.

After buying the land on Brawley, in January of 2019 we started getting the plans drawn up. This took about four months, and during that time, Randy was busy getting bids for what the construction costs would amount to. When the numbers started coming back to us, I was a bit shocked, because the costs had nearly doubled since I had last built a store nearly twelve years earlier.

We started construction on June 19th, hoping to have it all done by year's end, with a plan for opening in January of 2020. This would be the biggest and most state-of-the-art store I had ever built, and we intended to ask Mario Andretti to show up for a huge attraction at the grand opening. I expected we would quickly build a large and reliable customer base in the new area, and I was real excited going into this. Everything started well, but after a few months we began hitting obstacles like weather problems and getting the right kind of wiring for our computer systems. It turned out that AT&T had wired up that whole shopping center for fiber optic, and none of our computer equipment could run on fiber. We did not find out about this until the store was nearly finished, and after a couple months of going back-and-forth with AT&T, we finally got them to put in hard wire for our equipment.

By the time we concluded that deal with AT&T, the earliest we could open would be April 1st, but at least everything was set to go. Wouldn't you know it, right at that time the scare with Coronavirus derailed all of our plans for a major Grand Opening event. After all we had been through, and with all the high expectations for more than a year, this was quite a disappointment for everyone. We got the beautiful new store opened. However, with no existing customer base in that area, and with the media scaring people from even coming out, for the first month our business was very slow. After some time, things began picking up. At the time of this writing, near the end of 2020, we are doing well, and the future is looking very good.

I am still not sure what I will do with the lot on Blythe and Herndon, but whenever I stop by to see how things are going with Armen down on Brawley, I cannot help but think back to the days when I started out at the old Weber location. That was in 1974, when I rented that old building and Reneé and I got busy starting what would eventually become *Goodguys Tire and Auto Repair*. By the way, Armen also runs the location we built next to that old building on Weber, and I am real proud of him, along with John Brownrigg and my son Scott, all of whom run the stores I have built over the past forty years.

As I mentioned way back in the Preface to this book, I want my story to show that when you put your time and effort and integrity into your dream, it can happen. Through the decades, I looked at each new location as my new opportunity to see where we could go next. *Goodguys*, the Management Agreement Program, and now this 12-bay store—it is all my dream that came true.

Throughout my career I did not do much reflecting on where I had come from and what I started with. I was always looking forward to the next opportunity, or to dealing with a challenge in the present. Going through life the way that I have, in the fast lane since my youth, I did not stop to take a careful look at what had been accomplished. Writing this book, on *My Life as I Remember It*, has given me the experience of looking at myself and my history in a mirror.

In business, as with life in general, I never had a written plan. I just knew that I wanted to be in business for myself, and that I wanted to provide my family with more than what I and my siblings had growing up. Along the way, through the good times and the bad, I never felt satisfied with what I had accomplished, but I always believed I could do better.

After traveling all over the world, I have learned that no country gives opportunity like America. But even here it is never easy to grow and expand a business. In the late 1980s, I lost my first love and best friend, right at a time when television and radio stations were calling me a crook because of a Bureau official who wanted to do a personal favor for a woman and get some attaboys in Sacramento. There were some really tough times, and you've got to have it in your gut to do what I did. I sacrificed a lot to get where I am, and I stayed the course through many ups and downs. I want my life story to show that by sacrificing your time, investing your money wisely, and by sticking with principle and putting sweat and backbone into your life and work, YOU can build your own success from the ground up.

By way of encouragement, and not as a boast, I want to remind the reader that I had no formal education beyond high school, and no professional training in building and running a business. I have worked for everything I have gotten, and I never drew a nickel from unemployment or any kind of government subsidy. A lot of people have said to me how lucky I am to have had parents who passed this business on to me. Actually, as the reader will now know, my parents sent me away at age eighteen with twenty dollars in my pocket and a tank full of gas. This book was written to show that you do not have to be born with a silver spoon in your mouth to achieve success.

After coming to America penniless, an immigrant who could not speak a lick of English, at age thirty I took over a nearly bankrupt store and built an organization doing $30 million of business a year. After sharing a bedroom with four brothers and drinking milk from a cow in our back yard, I went on to sleep in the best hotels in the world and to eat in the best and most famous restaurants. From picking cotton, grapes, apricots and string beans for hours before school in the morning, and then until dark in the evening, I can now pick up a phone and have almost anything I want brought to my door. I flew the Goodyear blimp, rode with A.J. Foyt around the Indy 500 Speedway, hosted Mario Andretti in my hometown, and provided jobs for hundreds of people who needed employment. Today, in my seventies and in semi-retirement, I look back and think of the lives I have impacted, and how I have broken every challenge that I set for myself. But I lived so fast that I never stopped to look at all of this, or to really think about it.

Most of the history I have of my family is from what my father recorded and my sister, Lynda, transcribed and then translated from Russian. Had it not been for the recorder and the blank tapes that I bought for Father and showed him how to use, all that we would have of the history is our fading memories of old stories he reminisced to us. So, I wanted to put my own remembrances into writing, to preserve the history for my children, and for their children, and for the generations to come after them. During all those years I did not take notes, so this book has been written from what could be pulled out of my memories.

In closing, I would like to pass on the words of my father, who when all is said and done is the big hero in my life. At the end of his Memoirs, my father said:

> *So, with these words, I will finish up. Please listen to my story and take it to heart and live a good life. Be responsible, be accountable, and I encourage you to put your trust in God for everything and keep His ways.*

1972

2020

New opportunity

THE END?

Made in the USA
Las Vegas, NV
19 December 2020